THE POWER OF THE

SWORD

COMES IN LINE WITH THE LAW OF THE WORD

Developing Leaders
For the Work of Ministry

Kenneth Peters Jr.

The Power of the Sword Comes in Line with the Law of the Word

DEDICATION

This book is dedicated to the legacy of Kenneth Peters Jr.
Ken gave his life to bring a present-day reformation to the
body of Christ!

Ken went onto his heavenly home on August 14, 2021.

Ken and Tonja Peters

CONTENTS

"Wisdom is the principal thing;
Therefore, get wisdom.
And in all your getting, get understanding."
Proverbs 4:7 (NKJV)

FOREWORD

Throughout church history, ancient Christian leaders viewed the training and discipling of their followers as their sacred duty. It was considered customary for godly, gifted men and women to transfer both their acquired knowledge and their accumulated life skills to the next generation of followers. Failing to lovingly impart these instructions would be considered an unimaginable loss and dereliction of leadership duties. The apostle Paul models this in his clear admonition to his son in the faith, Timothy:

"You then, my son, be strong in the grace that is in Christ Jesus. And the things you have heard me say in the presence of many witnesses entrust to reliable people who will also be qualified to teach others." **(2 Tim. 2: 1-2 NIV)**

Today you hold in your hands a treasured gift! This leadership manual contains the distillation of decades of God's instruction, and the life lessons learned by our friend and mentor, Ken Peters. Much of what you have received as a gift, came at a high cost: radical obedience to God's call, a commitment to a daily life of faith and a relentless pursuit of knowing Father God with zealous love and devotion. This manual is not simply a collection of essential teachings; it is a clarion call to *you, and your own radical obedience to God's plans and purposes for your life.*

As you read and apply these lessons, I trust you will hear Ken's instructions and sense God's heart for you, royal child of God and my dear fellow disciple.

Steve Witmer

While reading this book, I began to hear a friend's voice sharing the Word, with familiar intonations and verbiage that were uniquely his. Anyone familiar with Kenneth Peters could recognize that his voice resonated with a serious passion for the Father. Because of the decades I spent listening to Kenneth minister, his voice was very familiar to me. As I read through the teaching material, suddenly, I realized it was no longer Kenneth's voice I was hearing; it was the voice of the Father. I began to weep with a deep desire to not only be with my old friend, but also with the Father. I realized this was not mere information being given to me, but I was being given an impartation to know Him, our Father, at a level at which I was not currently living. I was entering into a spiritual dimension that was not primarily informational, but a sphere that was designed for transformation. The chapters of this leadership manual are meant for transformation. This was not written for you to simply gather more information to further your ministry; it is a leadership path that is pointing you to a deep encounter with our heavenly Father.

Today many leaders are forfeiting their futures because they care more about their own popular reputation and success rather than their character. The current generation that is leading the Church, the Bride of Christ, primarily operates as orphans, fatherless. Malachi 4:5-6 shows the future leader will be a father who cares for his family. This is God's standard.

Kenneth has penned a manual that will help with the process of deepening one's personal commitment to God's standards, which includes demonstrations of God's power and the equipping to live these standards. Each chapter contains detailed prophetic applications that help provide a clearer more vivid picture of the Father's heart to influence and direct every person into their purpose and identity.

Emerging leaders will love the spiritual foundation the manual provides, experienced leaders will enjoy a new awareness of the importance of one's identity, mentoring leaders will want to use this manual to equip the next generation of leaders. If you are looking for a clear direction into Kingdom principles that build the proper mindset for you, your family, or team members, it's in your hands. All who use this manual will benefit from its wisdom.

Dr. Rocky Tannehill

Tannehill Capital Partners, LLC

Nashville, TN

We are privileged to be alive to witness these historic times. His church, the body of Christ, is being recalibrated to reflect Christ more fully to a dying culture. We see the emerging signs of another great awakening in the nations as the light of the Gospel invades the darkness. We see religion failing but beams of Kingdom light springing up in the most unlikely and previously hidden places. Like seasons past, we are beginning to see the Kingdom demonstrated in power and much assurance. We are on the cusp of the greatest harvest of souls the world has ever seen. God is in control; His plans will not be hindered.

More than ever, we need men and women who are prepared to lead in this great harvest and outpouring of the Holy Spirit. We need leaders fully trained in the work of the ministry, filled with the Holy Spirit, aligned with the Word, and who lead with godly character. We need leaders who are empty of self-ambition and glorify Christ alone. Are you called to lead? Do you want what God desires and to accomplish it in His greatness? Do you desire to align with the faith and spirit of fathers of the faith who have gone before? Then this teaching and preparation manual, inspired by the Holy Spirit, is for you!

It is my joy and privilege to have known the author of this manual, Kenneth Peters, his wife Tonja, and their family for nearly twenty-four years. With the gentleness of faithful servants of God, Ken and Tonja, through their prophetic gifts and lifestyle, have imparted teaching and delivered God's Word that has impacted individuals, congregations, denominations, regions, and nations. Their hallmark has been to devote their entire lives to the spiritual and practical growth of individuals and church communities, even through seasons of personal suffering. Kenneth's desire has always been to see people recognize the call of God in their lives and to live out that calling with Biblical integrity.

I was blessed to have witnessed Ken and Tonja lovingly minister through teaching, prophetic ministry, and counseling to thousands of high school students, parents, and staff over the years in the Christian school community where I served as principal. I have also had the privilege of ministering under Ken's leadership and prophetic mantle to various churches in Canada and Mexico. My wife Eleanor and I have considered them cherished friends. They are authentic Christ-followers and faithful, unwavering servants of God.

The Lord recently called Ken home to be with Him. Should the Lord delay His return, the fruit of Kenneth and Tonja's labors in the Kingdom will be evident for generations to come. May you be blessed and equipped as you read and apply the rich knowledge and wisdom shared by this mighty servant of God.

Paul Johnson

ACKNOWLEDGMENTS

I am thankful to my husband, Kenneth, who paved a way for so many individuals and leaders to live a life of freedom from the legalism and religion that kept us bound. Ken, you taught us that we could live a life filled with freedom submitted to the Holy Spirit, and to walk in our own personal authority!

Even though you are living on in eternity, I know you are peering down with the great cloud of witnesses cheering us on to keep going!! We will do just that! We will keep going until our race is finished. Thank you for all the breadcrumbs that you left behind to help others and me find the Way.

Thank you to my daughter, Candice Peters, for your endless editing. I'm sure Dad has his eyebrow raised at our formatting and changes, but I couldn't have completed this in excellence without you!

A huge thank you to Alex Delgado for capturing the vision of the power of the sword, you did an amazing job! I am grateful for your eye for design.

Finally, thank you to my dear friend, Doris Schmalz, for your encouragement, strength, and spiritual insight in navigating these pages.

Tonja Peters

HOW TO USE THIS BOOK

Although it could easily be studied alone, this book was originally written as a manual to be taught in a classroom setting. It was developed over many years of study, application, and ministry experience. While studying, be mindful of a few things. Bolded statements are used to show Ken's original emphasis on certain weighty ideas. Certain points are made to be discussed with others, while other sections are meant to encourage introspection and self-evaluation. If your desire is to grow in leadership, be honest with yourself and the Holy Spirit as you work through each chapter.

This manual was written and developed throughout many years at The Gathering @ Corona, the pilot church for a present-day reformation. There is a call from the heart of God for the Body of Christ to operate in the authority and fullness of His power, and there must be a response and reforming of what we know as "church." This must start with leaders, the men and women of God called to shepherd, develop, and equip believers. It is not through the leadership of singularity, but through the power of plurality that we will finally begin to operate as one. We have left references to The Gathering throughout the entirety of this manual; however, we invite you to utilize it for your own growth regardless of ministry title, church name, or denomination. The truths God revealed to Ken through diligent study of the Word are universal; they can and should be liberally applied.

SPIRITUAL LEADERSHIP
AN HONORABLE AMBITION

Most believers have reservations about aspiring to leadership. They are unsure about whether it is truly right for a person to want to be a leader. After all, is it not better for the position to seek out the person rather than the person to seek out the position? Has not ambition caused the downfall of numerous, otherwise great leaders in the church, people who fell victim to "the last infirmity of noble mind"? *(John Milton)*

William Shakespeare expressed profound truth when his Wolsey said to the English general:

> *"Cromwell, I charge thee, fling away ambitions,*
> *By that sin fell the angels, how can a man then,*
> *The image of his Maker, hope to profit by it?"*

No doubt, Christians must resist a certain kind of ambition and remove it from their lives! However, we must also acknowledge other ambitions as noble, worthy, and honorable! **These two verses provide both encouragement and a warning…**

> *1 Timothy 3:1 "To aspire to leadership is an honorable ambition." (NEB)*

1

Jeremiah 45:5 "Should you then seek great things for yourself? Do not seek them." (NIV)

When ambition carries out a burning desire to be effective in the service of the Lord, to realize God's highest potential for our lives we can keep both these verses in mind and hold them in a healthy tension. When the Apostle Paul wrote this to Timothy the times were much different than today where being a leader carries with it glamour, prestige, and privilege, and people aspire to leadership for reasons quite unworthy and self-seeking. When Paul called a leader, it was considered an honorable calling because of its servanthood, suffering, deep commitment to the difficulties of persecution, and great danger of losing one's life. **Holy ambition has always been surrounded by distortions.** Paul tells us that leading within the church is the most important work in the world. When our motives are right, this work pays eternal dividends; only a deep love for Christ and genuine concern for the church can truly motivate people to be leaders.

Jeremiah was not condemning all ambition as sinful, but he was pointing to selfish motivation that makes ambition wrong, "great things for yourself." **Desiring to excel is not a sin.** Motivation determines ambition's character! Jesus never taught against the urge to high achievement, but He did expose and condemn unworthy motivation.

Philippians 2:3 "Be sure to never act out of selfish ambition." (TNT)

Galatians 5:19-20 "The self-life will manifest itself in such works as these divisions, jealousy, outburst of anger, selfish ambition, dissentions to authority, party factions, envy..." (TNT)

2

Philippians 1:15-16 "It is a sad fact that some preach Christ out of wrong motives of selfish ambition, envy, and rivalry; but others lead out of right motives, seeking the good of those whom they witness to. They share the truth in love…" (TNT)

All believers are called to develop God-given talents, to make the very most of their lives, and to develop to the fullest their God-given gifts and capabilities! **Ambition that centers on self is sinful.** However, ambition that centers on the glory of God and the welfare of His church is a mighty force! True greatness, true leadership, is found in giving yourself in service to others, not coaxing or manipulating others to serve you.

"One of the outstanding ironies of history is the utter disregard of ranks and titles in the final judgments men pass on each other, the final estimate of men shows that history cares not one iota for the man or title a man has borne, nor his office he has held, but only the quality of his deeds and the character of his mind and heart." Samuel Brengle; Salvation Army Leader

"Let it once be fixed that a man's ambition is to fit into God's plan for him, and that he has a North Star ever in sight to guide him steadily over any sea, however shore-less it seems. He has a compass that points true in the thickest fog and fiercest storm, and regardless of magnetic rocks." S. D. Gordon

"I have one ambition: it is He and He alone." Count Nikolaus Von Zinzendorf

For Thought and Consideration:

1. How would you illustrate the differences between self-centered and God-centered ambition for your own life?

2. Who has most influenced you toward the example of godly leadership?

3. What are some areas of honorable/holy ambition in your life?

THE MASTER'S MASTER PRINCIPLE: SERVANTHOOD!

Mark 10:43-44 "...Whoever wants to become great among you must be your servant, and whoever wants to be first must be slave of all." (NIV)

Given the importance of competent leaders in the church we might expect that the Bible would use the term more often. In fact, the King James Bible uses leader only six times. Found much more often is the role of servant. We do not read about "Moses, My leader," but "Moses, My servant."

This is exactly what Jesus taught us. Jesus was a revolutionary, not in a guerilla warfare sense, but in His teaching on leadership. He overturned the existing order! In the world's ears the term servant spoke everywhere of low prestige, low respect, and low honor. Most people were not attracted to such a low-value role. **When Jesus used the term, however, it was synonymous with greatness and that was a revolutionary idea. It still is!**

Christ taught that the Kingdom of God was a community where every member serves others. He defined the ultimate purpose using that term:

> *Mark 10:45 "For even the Son of Man did not come to be served, but to serve, and to give His life as a ransom for many." (NIV)*

Paul wrote in the same spirit, *"...serve one another humbly in love." (Galatians 5:13 NIV)* Our loving service should also spread to the needy world around us, but in most churches a few people carry most of the load.

5

Jesus knew that the idea of a leader as a "loving servant of all" would not appeal to most people, but "servant" is still His requirement for those who want to lead in His kingdom! We see a sharp contrast between what the world views as leadership and what the Lord does.

Mark 10:42-43 "Not so with you…" (NIV)

Even James and John, who were very close to Jesus, tried utilizing the world's concept for promotion and leadership, but Jesus did not give an inch to their campaign for office. (*Matthew 19:28, Matthew 20:22*) Jesus responded that they didn't know what they were asking for. James and John wanted the glory, but not the cup of shame; the crown, but not the cross; the role master, but not servant. Jesus used this occasion to teach us **two great principles of leadership** that we must never forget.

1. The sovereignty principle of spiritual leadership

> *Mark 10:40 "but to sit at My right or left is not for Me to grant. These places belong to those for whom they are prepared." (NIV)*

> A more common reply might have been, "honor and rank is for those who have prepared themselves for it and worked very hard to get it." Jesus' teaching was fundamentally different to earning a place. God assigns places of spiritual ministry and leadership in His sovereign will as He chooses! Effective spiritual leadership does not come as a result of theological training or seminary degree, as important as they may be. Jesus told His disciples, *"You did not choose Me, but I chose you and appointed*

you..." (John 15:16 NKJV)

The sovereign selection of God is designed to give great confidence to Christian workers. We can truly say, "I am here neither by the selection of an individual nor the election of a group but by the almighty appointment of God Himself."

2. The suffering principle of spiritual leadership

Mark 10:38 "...Can you drink of the cup I drink and be baptized with the baptism I am baptized with?" (NIV)

There is no hedging here, no dodging the issue and hard realities. Jesus simply set forth the cost of serving in His leadership! If the disciples figured they would learn about leadership on the fast track and appropriate perks and bonuses, they were soon disillusioned by Jesus' teaching and example. What a shock it was to discover that greatness comes through servanthood, and leadership through becoming a slave of all.

THE SPIRIT OF SERVANTHOOD

Dependence

True servants are dependent upon their Master!

Isaiah 42:1-4 "Behold! My Servant whom I uphold..." (NKJV)

Approval

God takes great delight in those who delight in pleasing Him.

Isaiah 42:1 "My chosen one in whom I delight..." (NIV)

Modesty

God's true servant conducts ministry that is not flamboyant but is nearly self-effacing.

Isaiah 42:2 "He will not cry out, nor raise His voice, nor cause His voice to be heard in the street." (NKJV)

Empathy

The Lord's servant is sympathetic with the weak, mercifully understanding towards those who err. How often have we seen the tread marks of fellow believers upon those who have fallen?

Isaiah 42:3 "A bruised reed He will not break, and smoking flax He will not quench; He will bring forth justice for truth." (NKJV)

Optimism

Pessimism and leadership are at opposite ends of life's attitudes. Hope and optimism are essential qualities for the servant of God who battles with the powers of darkness over the souls of men and women.

Isaiah 42:4 "He will not fail nor be discouraged, till He has established justice in the earth; and the coastlands shall wait for His law." (NKJV)

Anointing

None of these leadership qualities- dependence, approval, modesty, empathy, or optimism- is sufficient for the task. Without the oil of the supernatural, the touch of the Holy Spirit, these qualities are as dry as dust. *(Acts 10:38)* Are we greater than our Master? Can we do effective ministry without the Spirit of God working through us at every step? God offers us the same anointing He gave Jesus!

Isaiah 42:1 "I have put My Spirit upon Him; He will bring forth justice to the Gentiles." (NKJV)

For Review:

1. How can you tell when you are being a servant?

2. What examples would you use to explain the two principles of leadership to someone?

3. Which six characteristics in Isaiah 42 do you find a challenge to use in your leadership?

CAN YOU BECOME A LEADER?

Read Numbers 13:1-3

Eight essential qualities of leadership:

- Discipline, vision, wisdom, decision, courage, humility, integrity, and sincerity

Numbers 13:2 "Send men to spy out the land of Canaan, which I am giving to the children of Israel; from each tribe of their fathers, you shall send a man, everyone a leader among them." (NKJV)

When Jesus selected leaders, He ignored every popular idea of His day (and ours) about what kind of person could fit the role. Jesus' band of disciples started out untrained and without influence, a motley crew for world change. Today's group might have included a star-studded cast of directors and advisers, prominent statesmen, financiers, athletes, professors, or famous ministers.

Instead, Jesus chose from the ranks of workers, not professional clergy. Jesus chose people with little education, but they soon displayed remarkable qualities. He saw in them something no one else did, and under His skillful hand they emerged as leaders who would shock the world. To their hidden talents were added fervent devotion and fierce loyalty, developed in the school of failure and fatigue.

Natural leadership qualities are important; too often these skills lie dormant and undiscovered. If we look carefully, we should be able to detect leadership potential. If we have it, we should train it and use it for Christ's work.

Let's investigate your potential:

How do you identify and deal with bad habits? To lead others, you must master your appetites.

How well do you maintain self-control when things go wrong? The leader who loses control in adversity forfeits respect and influence; they must be **calm in crisis and resilient through disappointment.**

To what degree do you think independently? A leader must use the best ideas to make decisions; and cannot wait for others to make up his mind.

How well do you handle criticism? When have you profited from it? A humble person can learn from petty criticism and even from malicious criticism.

Can you turn disappointment into a creative new opportunity? What three actions could you take facing any disappointment?

> Go over it
> Get over it
> Get on with it

Do you really gain the cooperation of others and win their respect and confidence? **Genuine leadership doesn't need to manipulate or pressure others.**

Can you exert discipline without making a power play? Are your corrections and rebukes clear without being destructive? True leadership is an internal quality of the spirit and needs no show of external force.

In what situations have you been a peacemaker? A leader must be able to reconcile with opponents and make peace where arguments have created hostility.

Do people trust you with difficult and delicate matters?

Can you influence people to happily do some legitimate thing that they would not normally wish to do? **Leaders know how to make others feel valued.**

Can you accept opposition to your viewpoint or decision without taking offense? **Leaders always face opposition.**

Can you make and keep friends? Your circle of loyal friends is an index of your leadership potential.

Do you depend on the praise of others to keep you going? Can you hold steady in the face of disapproval and even temporary loss of confidence?

Are you at ease in the presence of strangers?

Do you get nervous in the office of your superior? **A leader knows how to exercise and accept authority.**

Are people who report to you generally at ease? **A leader should be sympathetic and friendly.**

Are you interested in people? All types? All races? No prejudice?

Are you tactful? Can you anticipate how your words will affect a person? **Genuine leaders think before speaking.**

Is your will strong and steady? Leaders cannot vacillate, cannot drift with the wind. Leaders know the difference between conviction and stubbornness.

Can you forgive? Do you? **Do you nurse resentments and harbor ill feelings toward those who have injured you?**

Are you reasonably optimistic? **Pessimism and leadership do not mix. Leaders are positively visionary.**

Have you identified a master passion such as that of Paul, who said, "this one thing I do!" Such singleness of motive will focus your energies and powers on the desired objective. Leaders need a strong focus!

How do you respond to new responsibility?

How we handle relationships tells us a lot about our potential for leadership:

Do other people's failures annoy or challenge you?

Do you use or cultivate people?

Do you direct or develop people?

Do you criticize or encourage people?

Do you shun or seek out the person with a special need or problem?

This self-examination means little unless we act to correct our deficits and fill in the gaps of our training. Perhaps the real test of leadership is whether you sit on the results or do something about it. Why not take the results and go into some intentional character training with Holy Spirit, the Spirit of discipline, and concentrate on strengthening those areas of weakness and correcting faults.

Jesus displayed desirable qualities in all fullness. Each Christian should make it a constant prayer that Christlikeness might more rapidly be incorporated into their personality.

Adding leadership potential to our lives usually requires that we shake off negative elements that hold us back.

> If we are overly sensitive when criticized and rush to defend ourselves, that must go.

> If we make excuses for failures and try to blame others or circumstances, that must go.

> If we are intolerant or not flexible with creative people, that must go.

> If we are disturbed by anything short of perfection in others, or ourselves, that must go.

> If we cannot keep a secret, we must not try to lead.

> If we cannot yield a point when someone else's ideas are better, we must not try to lead.

> If we want to maintain an image of infallibility, we must find something else to do besides leading people.

For Reflection:

1. Read again the leadership measurements; put a + or – beside each one as it applies to your present exercise of leadership.

2. How would you answer the title of the lesson?

3. What was the most convicting, challenging, or surprising thought in this lesson?

THE SEARCH FOR LEADERS

Psalms 75:6-7 "For exaltation comes neither from the east nor from the west nor from the south. But God is the Judge: He puts down one and exalts another." (NKJV)

"Give me a man of God- one man. One mighty prophet of the Lord, and I will give you peace on earth, bought with prayer and not a sword." (George Liddell)

Real leaders are in short supply. Constantly people and groups search for them. A question echoes in every corner of the church, "who will lead?" Throughout the Bible, God searches for leaders too.

> *1 Samuel 13:14 "But now your kingdom shall not continue. The LORD has sought for Himself a man after His own heart, and the LORD has commanded him to be commander over His people, because you have not kept what the Lord commanded you." (NKJV)*

> *Jeremiah 5:1 "Run to and fro through the streets of Jerusalem; See now and know; and seek in her open places if you can find a man, if there is anyone who executes judgment, who seeks the truth, and I will pardon her." (NKJV)*

The Bible shows us that when God does find a person who is ready to lead, to commit to full discipleship, and take on responsibility for others, that person is used to the limit. Such leaders will have shortcomings and flaws, but despite those limitations, they serve God as spiritual leaders. Such were Moses, Gideon, and David.

To be a leader in the church has always required strength and faith beyond merely average. **Why is the need for leaders so great, and the candidates so few?** Every generation faces stringent demands of spiritual leadership, and unfortunately most turn away. However, God welcomes the few who come forward to serve.

The church is painfully in need of leaders... real leaders! If the world is to hear the church's voice today, leaders are needed who are authoritative, spiritual, and sacrificial. Authoritative, because people desire reliable leaders who know where they are going and are confident in getting there. Spiritual, because without a strong relationship to God, even the most attractive and competent person cannot lead people to God. Sacrificial, because this trait follows the model of Jesus, who gave Himself for the whole world.

Churches grow in every way when they are guided by strong, spiritual leaders with the touch of the supernatural radiating in their service. The church sinks into confusion and impotence without such leaders! Today, those who preach with majesty and power are few, and the booming voice of the church has become a pathetic whisper. Leaders today, those who are truly spiritual, must take to heart their responsibility to pass on the torch to younger people as a first line duty.

Many people regard leaders as naturally gifted with intellect, personal forcefulness, and enthusiasm. Such character qualities certainly enhance leadership potential, but they do not define the spiritual leader! True leaders must be willing to suffer for the sake of objectives great enough to demand wholehearted obedience. Spiritual leaders are not elected, appointed, or created by committees of church assemblies. God alone makes them. One does not become a spiritual leader by merely filling an office, taking course work on the subject, or resolving in one's will to do the task. A person must qualify to be a spiritual leader.

Often truly authoritative leadership falls on someone who years earlier dedicated themselves to practice the discipline of seeking first the Kingdom of God. Then, as that person matures, God confers a leadership role, and the Spirit of God goes to work through him. When God's searching eye finds a person qualified to lead, God anoints that person with the Holy Spirit and calls him or her to a special ministry. *(Acts 9:17; 22:21)*

"It is not worn by promotion, but many prayers and tears. It is attained by confession of sin, and much heart-searching and humbling before God; by self-surrender, a courageous sacrifice of every idol, a bold uncomplaining embrace of the cross, and eternally looking unto Jesus crucified. It is not gained by seeking things for ourselves, but like Paul, by counting those things that are gain to us as loss for Christ. This is a great price, but it must be paid by the leader whose power is recognized and felt in heaven, on earth, and in hell." Samuel Brengle

God wants to show such people how powerful He really is! Not all who aspire to leadership are willing to pay such a high personal price. *(2 Chronicles 16:9)*

One last word of warning… If those who hold influence over others fail to lead toward the spiritual uplands, then surely the path to the lowlands will be well worn; people travel together; no one lives detached and all alone. We dare not take lightly God's call to leadership in our lives!

For Thought and Consideration:

1. God took eighty years to prepare Moses for his leadership task. In what ways has God been preparing you?

2. As you heard this study, what did you understand as the primary qualifying traits of godly leadership?

3. How are you affected by the closing warning in this study?

LEADING IN A CLIMATE OF FEAR AND UNCERTAINTY

Be a visible presence.

People are looking to us. People need assurance that we are working on their behalf. Do they see us rally to their cause? Make entry into their hearts.

Use clear communication.

We must speak unifying messages from us to them. "The only thing we have to fear is fear itself." (Franklin D. Roosevelt) Teach more faith filled truths than usual.

Offer credible hope.

Leaders deal in hope. Leaders point to "the best yet to come." Mix hope with substance (testimonies). Offer optimism with a real plan.

Make difficult decisions.

Accept the tough calls. Do your homework, don't make panicky or reactionary decisions. Seek counsel. Recognize your emotions and get a handle on them.

Personal renewal is key.

Master your own mind and thoughts before helping others do so. Rest and relaxation with others and with God. Look to the Word for refreshment. Stay in His presence for strength.

LEADING YOUNG LEADERS

Don't stereotype young leaders.

> Not all of them have entitlement mentalities. Not all of them are lazy. Not all of them need motivation.

Tell young leaders the truth.

> Be honest with them about their performance. Bring them on the inside. Give them opportunities. Stay current with them.

Protect young leaders.

> Protect their personal and family life. Protect them from power brokers. Carry weight with them.

Empower young leaders (really).

> Give them authority and autonomy, require accountability from them, then evaluate them.

Develop young leaders.

> This is an investment in their growth. Provide books and getaways for them and fellowship with them.

Include young leaders.

> Include them in conversations. Include them in meetings with dignitaries. Ask them questions. Initiate their input and release their gifts.

TODAY MATTERS: GUARANTEES FOR TOMORROW'S SUCCESS

Focus on today, not tomorrow. Jesus Christ *(Matthew 6:34)*

Today's attitude gives me possibilities.

Today's priorities give me focus.

Today's health gives me strength.

Today's family gives me stability.

Today's thinking gives me advantage.

Today's commitment gives me tenacity.

Today's finances give me options.

Today's faith gives me peace.

Today's relationships give me fulfillment.

Today's generosity gives me access.

Today's values give me direction.

Today's growth gives me potential.

Focus on making today the most important day you have.

THE GATHERING LEADERSHIP

Our vision is to do what God desires and to accomplish it in His greatness!

As a leadership team God wants to increase our level of maturity so that we can get to the place He has for us. What is that place? Where is that place?

It is our birthright; grasping who God really is, seeing Him as He is, fellowshipping with Him, being His special chosen people who know His nature, friendship, strength and even His heart. It is ours to know the weight of His glory, a habitation within us, where God's presence remains with us, a tangible weight felt each time we call upon His Name, to be great before our God!

As a team we shall learn to walk Christ-like in and through relational difficulties! This is our step into the new level of maturity the Lord has for us as leaders.

The Lord is giving us eyes to see the importance of the call over The Gathering. Blindness through self-motivation and the importance of personal ministry will no longer hinder our vision of the calling on the house.

The Lord is enabling us to function well with the extreme liberty extended to us through His leadership by growing our submission and obedience to the Holy Spirit and then even to His appointed leaders as well.

God has made very clear parameters around us to enable us to live safely and securely in His Kingdom. The Lord has given us greater abilities to self-govern our liabilities. The Lord is releasing to us a correct view of our place in ministry.

We can lose the correct view through:

> Self-inflation and wrong perceptions of our accomplishments. It's by grace alone.

> Blindness to the realization that our accomplishments while here at The Gathering are based upon being under the umbrella of The Gathering.

> Failure to be dependent upon the Lord's call over the house and to understand this fact is non-negotiable. If this is not understood, it can lead to an Absalom heart. *"If I were king..."*

> Failing to realize the truth that our calling here at The Gathering is for our good, for our development, for the process of humility, to gain a greater love for God and His people, and to learn to lead **in** Christ.

We are not here to build a ministry- this is a wrong perception. We are here to learn to relate to God's people, to learn to follow those over us, and in doing so we will be building alongside the Lord Jesus Christ His Kingdom. **We represent Jesus to the congregation!**

Areas the Holy Spirit is working on:

Those who seldom or never say, "I was wrong" or "I am sorry"

Those who regularly criticize others

High control people who cannot tolerate different points of view

Those who interpret suggestions as a personal attack and personal rejection

Those struggling with feelings of bitterness and resentment towards others

Those who serve faithfully and tirelessly but rarely take care of themselves

Those who are seldom or never transparent about struggles and difficulties

God chooses, calls, and equips leaders for His people! Every government has a head, without a head, government does not function well! Headship is the place of authority. Christ is the head of the church. Christ's headship is His authority, His lordship, His rulership, and His kingship. *(Colossians 1:20-22; Isaiah 9:6-7)* Authority structure determines the local church decision-making process, growth limits, and leadership philosophy. Christ is the head of The Gathering, yet He governs through chosen, qualified leaders He has ordained for the task! The Gathering is accountable for the souls God gives it.

The Gathering is a dwelling place for God's presence, a

vehicle for the moving of the Holy Spirit, a spiritual school where people are loved, restored, taught, equipped, and released into their God given purposes.

Leaders need to be birthed into:

The vision of the house

The principles of the house

The philosophy of the house

The standards of the house

The doctrines of the house

The procedures of the house

The spirit of the house

As the vision and the principles are set forth, they must be assimilated into the team member's spirit, not just their mind. A spiritual illumination must take place resulting in a teachable spirit and a changed leader.

LEVELS

Four points about new levels:

1. Your ability to utilize information contextually determines your level.

   This means you're able to hear God and put it into context in your life, be not hearers only. Take what you hear whether preached, sung, spoken, or read and say, "This belongs in my life!" If it is just church stuff that lives in here, and you can't make it work out there, then you level off.

2. The principles and policies you live by determine your level.

   Everybody administrates their life in a certain way. If you don't live by principles, you're going to live by circumstances. You have got to make a shift! You have got to shift from living your life based upon your circumstances to living your life based upon your principles. When you live your life by principles, you're not always moving, trying to adjust your life to your circumstances. **You must find and establish principles, policies, and procedures that are non-negotiable, cannot be bought, and that you will not change for convenience!**

   You will find when you go from level to level, there are principles and policies that you had in Egypt, some things that were acceptable in Egypt, some things that were ok in the wilderness, that are not ok once you get to the place of promise. To be successful, we must easily adjust to a new, higher standard of principles.

3. The general direction of your thoughts and energies determines your level.

> Say, "general." Don't miss this! Your level is determined by the general direction of your thoughts and energy! Anybody can have a really good day; one good day does not count when it comes to a level, it is just a good day in a bad place. Anybody in Egypt can have a birthday and be happy for a day, but you're still in Egypt. **Generally speaking,** you are either optimistic or pessimistic, this is what determines a new level! Are you getting this now?
>
> **Generally speaking, you're either** victorious or defeated, happy or sad, focused on your future or focused on your past.
>
> Energy follows fault, and you only have so much energy to bring to life. If your energy is focused towards yesterday- sad, depressed, pessimistic, frustrated- then you don't have enough energy to feed your future potential. You are starving your tomorrow because your past is still hungry. Somehow, you have got to starve your past and take what you are feeding it, and push it over into your dream, and start feeding where you are going rather than where you have been. Come on, are you getting this!!!!

4. The ability to fortify your deficits determines your level.

> Everybody that breathes air has deficits and weaknesses, everybody that's breathing air has blind spots, everybody that's breathing air has something

30

they're not good at, everybody that's breathing air needs a little help now and then, so everybody has deficits in life. Your level will begin to move when you figure out how to fortify your deficits! When you figure out "just because I can't do this, or just because I can't do that, or just because this happened, I am not going to allow that to be the defining factor of my life." If not, those statements can become an escape route, the excuse used for never achieving the promise that God has for you.

The Bible says, "Jacob leaned on his staff." *(Hebrews 11:21)* Sometimes you have to have someone around that you can lean on because you're not strong in a certain area. Two are better than one, and a three-fold cord is not easily broken. Partner with somebody who is strong where you are weak. Don't hook up with someone weaker than you because they can't help you and you can't help them; you will both fall. Lean on someone with stability of character, someone with a settled, untroubled heart that cannot allow offense.

A man who manipulates himself into a place of leadership without serving is a leader who will manipulate the body of Christ. **All potential ministry leaders must encounter the revealing fire of God. Fire reveals the true nature of the potential leader. Until a leader goes through the fire, he is an unknown factor in the leadership team.**

The New Testament specifically lists several ministry functions of the eldership. Elders govern the local church in all matters of doctrine, morality, church discipline, and financial integrity.

The Set Man or senior elder/pastor of the Gathering sets the vision or direction of The Gathering. His eldership team does not originate the vision but shares partnership with him in setting it. **Set, not determined!** Elders protect the church from a tyrant-ruling pastor who hires, fires, and dominates people!

The staff ministries of The Gathering work in partnership with the entire eldership. Staff ministries are under direct oversight of the senior elder/pastor. The senior elder/pastor has authority to hire or release staff ministries with the eldership. Yet, while the senior elder/pastor retains this authority, he is wise to involve the eldership in key staff decisions, to benefit from their wisdom and their knowledge of the people involved.

If the senior elder/pastor releases someone from the staff and from the eldership, then it becomes an eldership matter. If a staff member is released by the senior elder/pastor and the staff member feels he has a genuine grievance or has been treated unfairly, he may bring the matter to the eldership. This will keep a proper checks and balances system in place.

The eldership will be the final authority in all decisions regarding the purchasing or selling of lands or buildings as well as new building ventures.

AN ELDER IS...
THIRTY POINTS ON BEING AN ELDER

The following list includes ministry and other functions specifically given to elders in scripture.

1. An elder is to be an overseer.

   > *Acts 20:28 "Take heed therefore unto yourselves, and to all the flock, over the which the Holy Ghost hath made you overseers, to feed the church of God, which he hath purchased with his own blood." (KJV) (Also, 1 Peter 2:25)*

2. An elder is to be a ruler. (Greek word proistemi, to stand before, to preside, practice)

   > *1 Timothy 5:17 "Let the elders who rule well be counted worthy of double honor, especially those who labor in the word and doctrine." (NKJV) (Also, Romans 12:8, 1 Timothy 3:4, 5, 12; 5:17, 1 Thessalonians 5:12)*

3. An elder is to be a feeder.

   > *John 21:15 "So when they had eaten breakfast, Jesus said to Simon Peter, 'Simon, son of Jonah, do you love Me more than these?' He said to Him, 'Yes, Lord; you know that I love You.' He said to him, 'Feed My lambs.'" (NKJV)*

4. An elder is a prayer warrior.

   > *James 5:15-16 "And the prayer of faith will save the sick, and the Lord will raise him up. And if he has committed sins, he will be forgiven. Confess your*

trespasses to one another, and pray for one another, that you may be healed. The effective, fervent prayer of a righteous man avails much." (NKJV) (Also, Revelation 5:8; 8:3-4)

5. An elder is to be a watchman.

   Luke 12:37 "Blessed are those servants whom the master, when he comes, will find watching. Assuredly, I say to you that he will gird himself and have them sit down to eat and will come and serve them." (NKJV) (Also, 1 Thessalonians 5:6)

6. An elder is to be a student of the Word.

   2 Timothy 2:15 "Be diligent to present yourself approved to God, a worker who does not need to be ashamed, rightly dividing the word of truth." (NKJV) (Also 2 Timothy 3:16-17; Titus 3:9)

7. An elder is able to teach sound doctrine.

   1 Timothy 3:2 "A bishop must be blameless, the husband of one wife, temperate, sober-minded, of good behavior, hospitable, able to teach;" (NKJV) (Also, 2 Timothy 2:24; Titus 1:7)

8. An elder is to show compassion.

   2 Timothy 2:24-25 "And a servant of the Lord must not quarrel but be gentle to all, able to teach, patient, in humility correcting those who are in opposition, if God perhaps will grant them repentance, so that they may know the truth." (NKJV)

9. An elder is to be an example in all he is, all he says, and

all he does.

1 Peter 5:3 "Nor as being lords over those entrusted to you but being examples to the flock;" (NKJV)

10. An elder is to be a leader.

Hebrews 13:7 "Remember those who rule over you, who have spoken the word of God to you, whose faith follow, considering the outcome of their conduct." (NKJV)

11. An elder is called to sacrificial service.

Galatians 5:24 "And those who are Christ's have crucified the flesh with its passions and desires." (NKJV) (Also, Luke 14:25-33)

12. An elder is a wise counselor.

Proverbs 24:6 "For by wise counsel you will wage your own war, and in a multitude of counselors there is safety." (NKJV) (Also, Mark 15:43; Luke 23:50; Isaiah 9:16)

13. An elder is to work hard.

Philippians 2:25-30

14. An elder is to bear burdens.

Exodus 18:22 "And let them judge the people at all times. Then it will be that every great matter they shall bring to you, but every small matter they themselves shall judge. So, it will be easier for you, for they will bear the burden with you." (NKJV)

(Also, Deuteronomy 1:12; Galatians 6:5)

15. An elder is to be a team man.

   1 Corinthians 3:8-9 "Now he who plants, and he who waters are one, and each one will receive his own reward according to his own labor. For we are God's fellow workers: you are God's field; you are God's building." (NKJV)

16. An elder is to encourage the brethren.

   Galatians 6:1-2 "Brethren, if a man is overtaken in any trespass, you who are spiritual restore such a one in a spirit of gentleness, considering yourself lest you also be tempted. Bear one another's burdens, and so fulfill the law of Christ." (NKJV)

17. An elder is to share the same vision and promote unity in the church.

   1 Corinthians 1:10 "Now I plead with you, brethren, by the name of our Lord Jesus Christ, that you all speak the same thing, and that there be no divisions among you, but that you be perfectly joined together in the same mind and in the same judgment." (NKJV)

18. An elder is to be transparent.

   Proverbs 27:5-6 "Open rebuke is better than love carefully concealed. Faithful are the wounds of a friend, but the kisses of an enemy are deceitful." (NKJV)

19. An elder is to be submissive.

> *1 Peter 5:1-3 "The elders who are among you I exhort, I who am a fellow elder and a witness of the sufferings of Christ, and also a partaker of the glory that will be revealed; Shepherd the flock of God which is among you, serving as overseers, not by compulsion but willingly, not for dishonest gain but eagerly; nor as being lords over those entrusted to you, but being examples to the flock." (NKJV)*

20. An elder is to be a liberal giver.

> *2 Corinthians 9:1-6; 2 Corinthians 8:1-15; Malachi 3:4-12*

21. An elder is to have a positive attitude.

> *Philippians 2:14-15 "Do all things without complaining and disputing, that you may become blameless and harmless, children of God without fault in the midst of a crooked and perverse generation, among whom you shine as lights in the world." (NKJV)*

22. An elder is to lead a disciplined lifestyle.

> *Galatians 6:4 "But let each one examine his own work, and then he will have rejoicing in himself alone, and not in another." (NKJV)*

> *Proverbs 16:32 "He who is slow to anger is better than the mighty, and he who rules his spirit than he who takes a city." (NKJV)*

23. An elder is to be a man of faith, one who rises to the challenge.

1 Samuel 17:37 "Moreover David said, 'The Lord, who delivered me from the paw of the lion and from the paw of the bear, He will deliver me from the hand of this Philistine.' And Saul said to David, 'Go, and the LORD be with you!'" (NKJV) (Also, Joshua 1:1-16; Deuteronomy 32:20)

24. An elder is to be a worshipper.

Revelation 4:10-11 "The twenty-four elders fall down before Him who sits on the throne and worship Him who lives forever and ever, and cast their crowns before the throne, saying: 'You are worthy, O Lord, to receive glory and honor and power; For You created all things.'" (NKJV)

25. An elder is to protect the flock.

Acts 20:28-31

26. An elder is to be filled with the Holy Spirit.

Mark 1:8 "I indeed baptized you with water, but He will baptize you with the Holy Spirit." (NKJV)

27. An elder is to be motivated.

Proverbs 12:24 "The hand of the diligent will rule, but the lazy man will be put to forced labor." (NKJV)

28. An elder is to know his grace gift and his gift limitations.

Romans 12:3-9; 1 Corinthians 12:28; Ephesians 4:7-11; 1 Peter 4:10; 1 Timothy 4:14-15

29. An elder should listen to constructive criticism.

Proverbs 19:20 "Listen to counsel and receive instruction, that you may be wise in your latter days." (NKJV) (Also, Proverbs 19:27)

30. An elder is to practice loyalty.

Galatians 5:22 "But the fruit of the Spirit is love, joy, peace, longsuffering, kindness, goodness, faithfulness…" (NKJV)

WHY SHOULD THE GATHERING HAVE A LEADERSHIP TEAM?

Focus points for discussion:

All ministries have value before the Lord.

A one-man ministry presents limitations.

Bearing the burden alone exacts a price.

A one-man operation destroys leadership in others.

It is impossible for one person to meet the need of an entire flock.

A servant becomes great by making others successful!

Gathering team members should have:

A conviction that God has placed them where they are for His pleasure, His purpose, and for their good.

A conviction that places Christ and His people above all their own desires, ambitions, and opinions. Gathering team members must see ministry as a way to serve and to give rather than as a means to fulfill or promote themselves.

A willingness to accept any assignment necessary to advance The Gathering's overall vision. Gathering team members must reject position-consciousness, or an others should thank me, recognize me, or reward me attitude. As servants we become great by making others successful. Therefore, Gathering team members must come with a servant's spirit and a servant's heart having the overall vision of The Gathering in mind. We can never just serve in the areas we like or that we think will be the most fruitful and the most satisfying. We serve for the good of the whole body and the overall vision of the Lord for The Gathering.

A conviction of loyalty that will save The Gathering and the team in a time of testing. This conviction can only be proven when there is disagreement, disappointment, or disillusionment. This conviction keeps the larger picture in mind. Loyalty handles complaints and criticism easily because it understands the sad results of disunity and discord. Loyalty refuses to deny its commitment to others regardless of the cost. Loyal servants stand with those they are serving in their time of need. Loyalty and servanthood make great team members. Those who have these convictions always seem to have a lot of responsibility and are involved in many key areas of our fellowship. Remember, "The hair on the back of a good donkey is always worn thin."

A conviction of faithfulness will cause a team member to understand that promotion comes from the Lord, and the Lord promotes based on His principles. Faithfulness and integrity are basic principles for leadership. To be faithful in that which is least, qualifies a person to receive more. The reward of a job well done is another job.

A conviction of availability will cause team members to see availability as the needed ingredient to being a useful vessel to God, to other leaders, and to those being served. Being available requires good discipline of time and priorities. Availability is almost always more important than capacity.

SEVEN ESSENTIALS FOR THE GATHERING TO HAVE A WINNING TEAM

1. Winning leaders

   Winning leaders are those that clearly communicate vision that excites and empowers people, understand the source and proper use of power and authority, respond to the needs of others, have a high tolerance for experimentation, never condemn innovation, and are not insecure of others better than themselves.

2. Tangible goals

   The very word used in the New Testament for leader has to do with perception, focus, vision, and prophetic sight. We must have a vision, a mark to hit with real goals. We need to know where we are going and how we are to get there!

3. A "give-it-all-it-takes" attitude

   Clear vision and clear goals will create this attitude. Our communicated vision will cause others to put the needs of the whole before their own needs. This attitude will motivate our team beyond human levels of achievement. Sacrifice pleases God and releases His capacity for victory.

4. The ability to recover from failures

   Let's make a decision not to make a big deal out of our personal failures, failures of those on The Gathering teams, or even team failures. We must avoid the trap of falling into blame, accusation, and criticism when things go wrong. Examine our mistakes and the results honestly but avoid blame. We need to analyze how and why failure occurred, learn from it, encourage one another, and move on. Concentrate on the lesson learned not on failures.

5. Respect the value of a person as well as their talents and gifts

We all need to feel love and respect especially from those we love and respect! Peer level respect is worth more than gold and silver. We must continue to verbalize love and respect for team members. Consistent, sincere appreciation goes a long way in producing team spirit, (i.e., phone calls, notes, cards, and e-mails)

6. Intensity and excellence

Never allow victory to take the edge off spiritual hunger or alertness. The most dangerous moment comes with victory. Our team will keep the tension of prayer, the need for God, and humility after great victories.

7. Adherence to basic principles

Consistent practice of the basics is a must. Skill is kept by living within our principles. When we keep to the fundamentals, when adversity comes, we respond out of the overflow of values and guidelines that we've learned along the way. No crisis can overtake those who know the way.

Common problems to avoid in leadership:

The problem of doctrinal compatibility

The problem of disloyalty in attitude or action. Disloyalty is an attitude of the spirit.

The problem of philosophical differences that divide

The problem of prejudging actions by questioning motives

The problem of allowing disciples to praise some and devour others

The problem of becoming position minded

The problem of those who overestimate their own abilities and ministry

The problem of unmet expectations in relationships

The problem of ignoring standards and philosophies already established and agreed upon

THE GATHERING TEAM'S TWELVE BASIC PRINCIPLES

1. Be on time for appointments.

2. Be on time for prayer before services or at prayer meetings.

3. Be on time for leadership activities.

4. Be a participator in worship, not a spectator.

5. Be involved with as many weddings and funerals as possible.

6. Be faithful to attend public worship services.

7. Be conscientious of all reports and paperwork due.

8. Be connected, fervent, and enthusiastic in prayer and worship.

9. Be an example of hospitality.

10. Be a person of faith with a positive attitude.

11. Be a support to those preaching by taking notes and interacting.

12. Be approachable and available after services for God's people.

KEYS TO EFFECTIVE LEADERSHIP

Leadership ability determines our level of effectiveness and the potential impact of our church upon its members and our city. Success is within the reach of just about everyone, but success without leadership ability brings only limited effectiveness. The higher we are to climb the mountain the more we need leadership. The greater the impact you want to make, the greater the influence needs to be! The true measure of leadership is influence- nothing more, nothing less.

How can we cause people to desire to follow us? Create positive change, not short-term persuasion, but long-term influence that causes people to act on communicated vision! Hard work and godly character communicated through love causes others to follow! Volunteers cannot be forced to follow!

Trust is the foundation of leadership. To build trust as a leader you must exemplify these qualities: competence, connection, and character. Character makes trust possible, and trust makes leadership possible! Character communicates consistency, character communicates respect. People will tolerate our mistakes, but if we violate their trust, it is very difficult to regain.

"Leadership is a potent combination of strategy and character. If you must be without one, be without strategy." Norman Schwarzkopf

We don't build trust by talking about it. Trust comes by achieving results, always with integrity and in a manner that shows personal regard for the people with whom you work!

No man can climb beyond the limitations of his own character. When those we lead trust our character, they will also trust in our ability to release their potential. No strength within us, no respect given to us! Respect is earned by making sound decisions, admitting mistakes, and putting what's best for our followers ahead of our personal agendas. Kill preference!

Leaders touch a heart before they ask for a hand. People don't care how much you know, until they know how much you care! Be thoughtful. Cover up a great deal of your abilities with a desire to make others bigger than you so you can serve them, which makes it easier for those following to do something that needs to be done together! **To lead yourself use your head, to lead others use your heart.**

Only secure leaders give power to others. Empower others. **The best leader is the one who has sense enough to pick good people to do what he wants accomplished and the restraint to keep from meddling with them while they do it.** Some of the barriers to being secure are a desire for job security, resistance to change, lack of self-worth, and lack of knowledge of God's purpose for you.

People buy into the leader, then the vision. People don't at first follow worthy causes; they follow leaders who promote worthwhile causes! Every message that people receive is filtered through the messenger who delivers it. Have I given my people reasons to buy into me?

People want to go along with people they get along with! When followers don't like the leader, or the vision they look for a new leader. When followers don't like the leader, but they do like the vision, they still look for another leader. When followers like the leader, but not the vision, they change vision. When followers like the leader and the vision, they will get behind both.

Leaders understand that activity is not the only necessary approach. Good vision and a worthy cause are not enough! You must become a better leader; you must be able to get your people to commit to you. This is the price you have to pay if you want your vision to have a chance of becoming reality. Don't try to push the vision or agenda on people, allow them to catch it by seeing your credibility.

The leader's best friend is momentum. All leaders face the challenge of creating change in their area of oversight. The key to this change is working in and with momentum, not against the moving of the Spirit. Preparation releases motivation. Be set apart, spend time alone with God.

Effective inspiration, proper preparation, and consistent motivation create momentum. Momentum makes us look better than we are, and helps followers perform better than they are. Momentum is the proper agent for change; it's easier to steer than to start.

Leaders must give up to go up. We must be willing to give what we have been given to receive more! Our investing into others will only cause God to re-invest into us. Give and it shall be given unto you! Think of being reproducers. To add growth, lead followers. To multiply, lead leaders! The authority to lead is found in the authority to feed, **not from position or title!**

LEARNING TO HANDLE CONFLICT IN THE CHURCH

A leader who does not know how to handle conflicts will consistently have them. However, not all conflict is negative. Maturity is evidenced when a conflict is not encountered with overreaction, retaliation, or criticism. Conflict can make us hard or soft, bitter or better. Conflict strengthens our character. Conflict makes us examine and purify our motives. Conflict reveals faults and flaws in The Gathering and us. Conflict teaches us spiritual endurance and spiritual carefulness. At times, the Lord allows conflict to shake us so He can make needed changes!

Conflict defined is "a striking together, a contest, to fight, to clash, incompatibility, to be in opposition, sharp disagreement; emotional disturbance resulting from a struggle."

Conflict is a sister to contention. These two dwell together and grow together whenever they are not handled properly! Contention carries the idea of strife, quarreling, and rivalry.

Proverbs 6:16-19 "These six things the Lord hates: yes, seven are an abomination to Him; a proud look, a lying tongue, and hands that shed innocent blood, a heart that devises wicked imaginations, feet that are swift in running to mischief, a false witness that speaks lies, and he that sow's discord among brothers." (MEV)

Proverbs 18:18-19 "Casting lots causes contentions to cease and keeps the mighty apart. A brother offended is harder to win than a strong city, and contentions are like the bars of a castle." (NKJV)

James 3:16 "For where envying and strife is, there is

confusion and every evil work." (KJV)

Where there is contention and conflict there is also strife and discord!

Common leadership sources of conflict:

Inconsistency in the practicing of biblical principles that are clearly established at The Gathering

Leadership violating standards and attitudes taught to the people

Leadership presumptuously declaring vision or direction from the Lord and then aborting the direction without explanation

Leadership avoiding, procrastinating, or ignoring the need to confront those who are sowing seeds of contention, and then not properly handling the matter

The senior leader violating his own standards and wisdom in choosing unqualified leadership to serve the people, thus creating confusion

Leaders handling an explosive matter in haste, without prayer, and without considering ramifications of their actions or decisions

Leadership not consistently practicing the principle of forgiveness taught in Matthew 18, allowing offenses to grow at The Gathering and leaders

The senior elder violating the team spirit by acting independently of the elders or staff leadership in making major decisions which will affect the whole body

Practical tips in handling conflicts:

Refrain from hasty decisions.

Take immediate action with grace.

Allow for human failure.

Do not repeat half-truths.

Love looking for the best in people.

Discipline carnal impulses and negative reactions.

Handle vain imaginations.

Realize that we are at war with a spiritual adversary, the devil.

Allow some differences in methodology.

Deal with root problems not just manifestations.

All leadership should be underneath pushing up!

Ephesians 5:21 "Submitting to one another in the fear of God." (NKJV)

Struggles unique to the senior leader:

The senior leader/set man struggles with who he is supposed to be, who he wants to be, and who he has to be. The senior leader has to be a real person and approachable. Sometimes relationships bring disappointment. Understanding the struggles will free eldership to function well and cover well.

The set man wrestles with image.

The set man wrestles with relationships.

The set man wrestles with resentment.

The set man wrestles with expectations put on him.

The set man wrestles with priorities.

The set man wrestles with guilt at times.

The set man wrestles with the flesh.

The set man wrestles with emotions.

The set man wrestles with professionalism.

The set man wrestles with the limitations of his calling.

The set man wrestles with reality.

The set man wrestles with confidence.

The set man wrestles with tiredness.

The set man wrestles with role tension.

The set man wrestles with genuine fruitfulness.

The set man wrestles with discouragement.

The set man wrestles with judging others.

The set man wrestles with unanswered prayers.

The set man wrestles with the relentless march of time.

The set man wrestles with disappointments.

The set man wrestles with his own lack of Christlikeness.

Under pressure, ministers can find their attention shifting onto external goals and away from internal fruit in lives. Achieving more goals is seen as being fruitful, yet true fruitfulness is achieved in submission to the will of God.

THE LEADER'S CREED

People are unreasonable, illogical, and self-centered—
Love them anyway

If you do good people will accuse you of being selfish and
having an ulterior motive—
Do good anyway

If you are successful, you will win false friends and true
enemies—
Succeed anyway

Honesty and frankness make you vulnerable—
Be honest and frank anyway

The good you do today will be forgotten tomorrow—
Do good anyway

The biggest people with the biggest ideas can be shot down
by the smallest people with the smallest minds—
Think big anyway

People favor underdogs, but follow top dogs—
Fight for some underdogs anyway

What you spend building for years may be destroyed
overnight—
Build anyway

Give the world the best you have, and you'll always get
kicked in the teeth—
Give the world the best you have anyway

When you were born, you cried, and the world rejoiced. Let
the rest of your life be in such a fashion so that when you die,
the world cries and you rejoice.

Author unknown

MINISTRY TEMPTATIONS AND LEADERSHIP

To promote the highest end of ministry, the servant of God must begin with himself. Socrates once said, "The unexamined life is not worth living." Leaders, especially elders, must continually examine their lives before God and His Word.

Acts 20:28 "Therefore, take heed to yourselves and to all the flock, among which the Holy Spirit has made you overseers, to shepherd the church of God which He purchased with His own blood. (NKJV)

1 Corinthians 9:26-27 Therefore, I run thus: not with uncertainty. Thus, I fight: not as one who beats the air. But I discipline my body and bring it into subjection, lest, when I have preached to others, I myself should become disqualified. (NKJV)

"He who is required by necessity of his position to speak the highest things is compelled by the same necessity to exemplify the highest things." Gregory the Great

"Prayer, meditation, and temptation make a minister." Martin Luther

The longer we minister the more receptive we may become to certain hidden temptations.

> The temptation to become an administrator of things more than serving people out of love and our calling.

> The temptation to become mechanical and robotic with the things of God.

The temptation to coast on one's own spiritual maturity, thinking that leadership is equal to maturity, and being blinded by our own success and ministry accomplishments.

The temptation to seek material security as the basis for our joy and happiness.

The temptation to become hardened and distrusting towards people because of disappointments.

The temptation to find satisfaction in the failure of another leader, being motivated by ungodly jealousy amplifying our human nature and letting loose the hell within.

The temptation to measure ministry success by numbers, buildings, and budgets instead of the spiritual quality and maturity of the people.

The temptation to react against new truth because of who proclaims the truth.

The temptation to excuse little sins, habits, and shortcomings because of stress and sacrificial lifestyle.

The temptation to use people for personal gain, status, or goal accomplishment.

The temptation to function in ministry out of learned habits and principles instead of living out the life of Christ that comes only by abiding with Christ.

The temptation to allow the things of God to become too familiar so as to become presumptuous about sacred things.

"What lies behind us and what lies before us are tiny matters compared to what lies within us." Oliver Wendell Holmes

The Gathering wants to be an exciting church and to stay exciting, but life does not sustain this ideal. Every church has up and down times, times of revival and times of dryness. When we build the church on principles, seasons do not hinder our progress. People with principles obey the written Word of God with or without excited emotions. Principles guarantee longevity!

A principle is a guiding force, a comprehensive and fundamental law, doctrine. A trend is a current style or preference, something temporary. We cannot build on temporary, passing whims of human nature. Methods are many, principles are few; methods always change, principles never do! Principles are built on the Word of God. Methods can vary from leader to leader, from culture to culture, throughout time and generations, but principles are eternal anchors!

God's eternal principles are based on the eternal values as seen in the Word of God. They are an extension of God's character applied in any circumstance at any time and are derived from biblical history. They are usually evident within certain biblical models (tabernacle, priesthood, etc.) **God's eternal principles must become our convictions that conquer us and become our value system.**

Principles are an extension of biblical truths. Truth does not change! Methods are an extension of personality, style, culture, spiritual genes, etc. As leaders we must consistently evaluate and examine ourselves to make sure we do not compromise godly principles because of passion for success or growth. Methods can become like a barren woman, always unsatisfied. We must beware of trying to make methods better, more attractive, and more tolerable to humanistic, narcissistic culture. **A church, which lacks a solid foundation of basic principles, has no secure way to evaluate spiritual fads!**

Ask yourself these questions:

Am I responding to truth or trend?

Am I responding to personality or personal convictions?

Am I responding for spiritual reasons or selfish reasons?

Am I responding cautiously or hastily?

Three ingredients that move the church forward are basic biblical doctrines, biblical principles, and biblical methods.

The Dynamic Hub *(see diagram on page 61)*

Remember that the corporate body exists to express the life of God in community, as well as to release and benefit individual believers. Remember each believer exists to express the life of God, as well as to benefit the corporate good. **The objective rules the subjective. The clear interprets the obscure. The major emphasis rules the minor. Proven basics come before unproven ideas for success.** Better to build slowly with proven principles of

God's Word than risk it all in the name of innovation.

Let us commit ourselves to God's non-negotiable principles:

> The glory of God is the chief end of all men and women.
>
> The preaching of the Gospel is the preaching of the Kingdom.
>
> Scripture is the only normative authority for believers.
>
> Sin, salvation, and eternal death are eschatological realities.
>
> God desires all to be saved from sin and eternal death.
>
> God is the Supreme Ruler over His church, His servants. Everything is done in submission to Him.
>
> The Kingdom of God is the mission.
>
> The cross and resurrection of Jesus Christ are the source of Kingdom vision.
>
> The church is the vehicle for the Kingdom to be established.
>
> The Second Coming of Jesus is the motive that keeps the vision sure!

THE DYNAMIC HUB

Ephesians 4:11-16

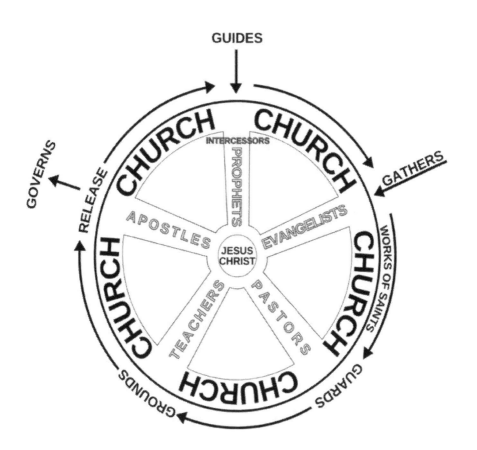

THE ELDERSHIP OVERSEEING/WORKING WITH THE FIVEFOLD MINISTRY TEAM

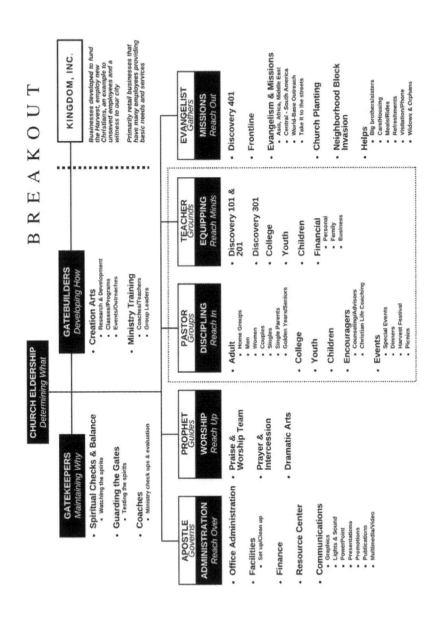

LEADERSHIP, CALLING, AND CHARACTER

PART I: FULFILLING OR FORFEITING YOUR CALL

Character is what God and the angels know of us. Reputation is what men and women think of us. Have you ever thought about what God sees when He looks into the depths of your life? What kind of person does He find you to be? Are you loving, generous, and hardworking, or are you bitter, angry, and self-gratifying? Who you are determines how you will respond to any and every situation, whether good or bad, positive or negative.

God's purpose for your life is a result of His foreknowledge, yet His divine will and plan for your life is conditional. It is based upon your cooperation. Every person has genuine options and as each choice is made, God responds accordingly. The freedom to fulfill God's design for your life is determined by your ability to choose options in light of your character. The future of all people lies in a measurable balance of God's sovereignty and human responsibility.

God is in control of all circumstances that may bear upon your life, but ultimately you are responsible for responding correctly, godly, and biblically to every circumstance good or bad. Your response in various situations will surely determine the character that you will possess. Regardless, if you are acting in love, forgiveness, bitterness, cold heartedness, happiness, joy, sorrow, or anger, your actions will affect the lives of those you lead.

Genesis 49:3-4 "Ruben, you are my firstborn, my might, the first sign of my strength, excelling in honor, excelling in power. Turbulent as the waters, you will no longer excel, for you went up onto your father's bed, onto my couch and defiled it." (NIV)

Great expectations had been formed of Reuben, but he refused to answer the call. Reuben was set to inherit a double portion of birthright and was in position to receive all the privileges associated with that title. However, the awful power of sensuality became Reuben's downfall. He had powerful passion, was uncontrolled, and wasn't self-governing!

Genesis 35:22 "While Israel was living in that region, Reuben went in and slept with his father's concubine Bilhah, and Israel heard of it." (NIV)

From Reuben we learn that sinful actions can remove people from leadership positions. Jacob described his son's character flaw as "turbulent waters." An unstable character, an unbridled will, and indulgence of passion brought down Reuben. He was a weak man who willed after his own desire. Like Reuben we may be born into greatness, but that is no guarantee of us becoming great.

It all comes down to character. We must understand that our lack of character development will also invade our future generations. Therefore, it is essential and critical to identify areas of weakness and commit to personal character development. Ask the Holy Spirit to shine the searchlight of Heaven on your character and reveal any areas that need deeper development.

Being prone to disloyalty, leading to divisiveness and rebellion *(Numbers 16)*

Being prone to spiritual and genetic weakness in leadership

Being prone to choose unwise actions, causing unnecessary reactions in others *(Numbers 32 and Joshua 22:10-20)*

Being prone to complacency, which divides the heart *(Judges 15:15-16 and Joshua 5:15-16)*

Being prone to selfishness and internal instability *(Judges 5:15-16)*

Being easily captivated by the enemies' snares causing detours from the fulfillment of vision *(Genesis 37:21-22)*

PART II: COMMITTED TO PERSONAL CHARACTER DEVELOPMENT

Personal character development is consistently overcoming areas of our lives that do not reflect the qualities of Jesus' leadership. The Lord cares about a leader's lifestyle and character, not just gifts and anointing. Gifts are freely given, while character development comes only with time and growth cultivation. Time and great personal effort bring forth godly character, this is why God invests time into His leaders, disciplining them, stretching them, and developing them to become vessels of honor.

Importance of Character

Long lasting, effective ministry must be built upon the foundation of Christ-like character. God is committed to however long it takes or how uncomfortable we may feel in the process, just as long as the outcome is growth. As a leader, it is your responsibility to submit and cooperate completely with the Holy Spirit's working in you to bring God the leader He desires. Character begins in the heart and must be cultivated to bring forth full fruit in action.

"If I take care of my character, my reputation will take care of itself." D.L. Moody

Defining Character

Character is the seat of our moral being.

Character reflects our inner life.

Character will reflect either the traits of God's nature or the sinful nature.

Character is influenced either by the Word of God or the world around us.

Character is displayed in our actions under pressure.

Character is the sum-total of all the positive and negative qualities in our life. (Influenced by my thoughts, values, motivations, attitude, feelings, and actions)

The original meaning of character was "a notch, identification, a scratching or writing on a stone, an embossed stamp made upon a coin or stone." The definition of character is "a distinctive mark impressed or formed by an outside or internal force upon an individual."

The Son is the radiance of God's glory and the exact representation of His being. *(Hebrews 1:3 NIV)* Jesus is the very character of God, the very stamp of God's nature, the one whom God imprinted His being upon. We are living stones, meaning God's character embossed upon us causes us to live in His light and likeness.

More on Character

Character is who we are at this present time. A person may act or think one way under the blessing of the Lord, but quite differently when the trials of life are his portion.

Character includes our inner thoughts, motives, and attitudes, not just outward actions. Thoughts, though hidden, indicate the real you, motives express your hidden man! To change our character, we must go deeper than our actions clear to the inner recesses of our hearts. *(Hebrews 4:12-13)*

Character does not appear without pressure. The common irritations of everyday life expose the weakness in our life! *(Romans 5:3-5)* The pressures of life test what the Lord has really accomplished in our character. Are we consistent when the heat is on or off?

Character is not only what people see on our outside, but also what cannot be seen. God sees the real person we are, He knows us as we really are. *(1 Peter 3:4)* Man may look at the external, but the Lord looks at the heart. *(1 Samuel 16:7)* We can do many outward spiritual works and still be quite ungodly inwardly. (Pharisees)

Character is not just having wisdom to comment on others behavior. A person with true character does not just tell others what to do, but lives as an example worthy of following. *(1 Timothy 4:12)* Are you worthy of following?

Character shows our godly principles in every situation towards all people. Character is not limited to our relationship between other believers. *(1 Timothy 3:7)* A Christian worker must show the same respect to an unbelieving employer. Character can be discerned by the way a leader respects and honors his father and mother. Character is not limited to our relationship with our spiritual family but must be the same with our natural family as well.

Character Assessment:

What is a man or woman of God?

What is God looking for in my leadership today?

What specific qualities must I have to be a balanced leader?

Am I a spiritual leader?

Self-evaluation time:

> Do I stay in close communion with the Holy Spirit?
>
> Do I completely accept the Bible as the Word of God?
>
> Do I love God's people?
>
> Do I willingly submit to authority from my heart?
>
> Do I love sinners and backsliders?
>
> Do I truly worship God with all my heart?
>
> Do I have a strong prayer life?
>
> Do I have a mature attitude in high-pressure situations?
>
> Do I let another person finish a job that I began without feelings of bitterness?
>
> Do I listen to and really receive correction and adjustment?
>
> Do I accept it when someone else is assigned a job for which I am better qualified?

Do I have inner peace during times of turmoil?

Do I forgive those who deliberately ignore me?

Do I control my anger?

Do I put others before myself?

Do I pass up certain present pleasure to achieve long-term goals?

Do I finish projects that I begin?

Do I freely admit when I am wrong?

Do I keep my promises and complete my commitments?

Do I hold my tongue when it is best to do so?

Do I accept and live in peace with the things I cannot change?

As the character of the world becomes more corrupt, the Lord is causing the character of His people to mature and reveal Him! This must be seen in our spiritual life, personal life, home life, social life, ministerial life, marriage life, and financial life.

Count the cost and pay the price:

Consider your goals and purpose in a realistic way.

Calculate how much energy and effort is needed to accomplish the task.

Anticipate distractions, hindrances, and difficulties that will be in your path.

Examine your privileges to see if they weaken or strengthen your resolve.

Covenant with yourself not to give up.

Connect yourself with those going the same direction.

Purpose in your spirit that it is God's way and God's timing that will prevail.

Remember our vision is to do what God desires and to accomplish it in His greatness!

WORDS OF ENCOURAGEMENT

Read Isaiah 41:8-15 and highlight these key words and phrases of encouragement in the passage:

"Chosen", "not rejected", "fear not", "I am with you", "I am your God", "I will strengthen you", "I will uphold you", "I will destroy your enemies", "I will make you My threshing instrument".

TWENTY RESOLVES THAT MARK YOU AS GOD'S LEADER

As a leader, you must run according to the non-negotiable resolves to which you are committed.

Make the decision today to uphold the following:

1. I resolve to govern my life by the principle of purity. *1 Corinthians 7:1, 9:27; 1 Peter 1:15-17; Romans 12:1-2; Philippians 4:8-9*

2. I resolve to govern my life by submitting to all levels of godly authority. *2 Corinthians 10:8; Matthew 7:29*

3. I resolve to hold my faith in God and His Word. *Joshua 24:15; Hebrews 4:12; 2 Timothy 3:16; Luke 16:17*

4. I resolve to hold on to the God thoughts coming to me every day. *Jeremiah 29:11-12; Psalm 85:8; John 10:27*

5. I resolve to hold my spirit above the words and ideas of men. *1 Timothy 1:6; 1 Corinthians 2:4-5; 1 Thessalonians 2:6-7; Romans 12:1-2*

6. I resolve to hold my vision to see beyond the immediate into the eternal. *2 Corinthians 4:17; 1 Corinthians 2:9-10*

7. I resolve to hold my faith perspective, seeing the best in the worst of times. *Daniel 3:16-18; Hebrews 11:1-3*

8. I resolve to hold relentless pursuit for true Biblical revival. *Hosea 10:12; Psalm 85:6*

9. I resolve to hold my passion for building an impactful local church. *Matthew 16:18-20; Acts 2:37-47*

10. I resolve to hold onto the mantle God is making for me. *1 Kings 19:16-21; 2 Kings 2:13-15; Jeremiah 17:10; Luke 9:62*

11. I resolve to hold on to the call of becoming a reformer in my generation. *Genesis 7:1; Judges 2:10; Esther 4:14*

12. I resolve to hold my covenant relationships all the days of my life. *2 Samuel 18:3; 2 Chronicles 23:1*

13. I resolve to hold an advancing spirit, rejecting any attitudes of retreat. *Exodus 14:16; Joshua 10:12-15; Philippians 4:8-11*

14. I resolve to hold my heart toward the harvest of lost souls and un-churched people. *John 4:35; Matthew 9:35-37*

15. I resolve to hold my God-given dream seeds by faith. *Proverbs 4:23, 13:12; Deuteronomy 1:21; Genesis 37:1-10*

16. I resolve to destroy all strongholds of my mind which hinder the work of God. *2 Corinthians 10:3-5; Romans 12:1*

17. I resolve to endure life's contradictions by faith and prayer. *2 Corinthians 6:1-4; James 4:7-10*

18. I resolve to steadfastly hold to my commitment to see miracles and the supernatural today. *Hebrews 13:8; Judges 6:13; 1 Corinthians 12:10, 28; Galatians 3:5*

19. I resolve to hold a forgiving spirit to all, for anything, at all times. *Matthew 6:14-15, 18:21-22, 32-34; Hebrews 12:15; Ephesians 4:30-32*

20. I resolve to hold my integrity as the most important achievement of life and ministry. *Genesis 20:5-6; 1 Kings 9:4; Job 27:5; Psalm 25:21, 78:72; Proverbs 10:9*

ELDER AND DEACON TRAINING
THE CHURCH ELDERSHIP: A PRIVILEGE AND A TRUST

If someone wants to be an elder member, a good guiding principle is that they should not become one. If someone tries to be an elder member, they definitely should not become one. Think about it, any board you've served on – you were asked to serve, and like most of us you gave it a lot of thought and prayer and probably tried to turn it down. Being nominated, selected, or invited is very different than seeking the position. Once someone has accepted a position, a desire to remain in that leadership is a different issue as long as that desire is about service and not power!

As long as your leadership is good enough to help The Gathering, you belong on the leadership team. However, if the church ever outgrows your ability to lead, you will have to step down. The purpose of your leadership is to serve the church and your pastor, not for the church or him to serve you! **Don't step up unless you're ready and willing to step down.**

Qualifications of Spiritual Leaders

1 Timothy 3:2-13 This passage sets the bar high!

In Paul's list of qualifications for church leaders, 1 Timothy 3:10 is key: *"But let these also first be tested."* Every leader should be tested before being given an official position. The preparation of a leader is crucial to their success. This is Paul's logic concerning leadership:

> **Leader's salvation-** Leadership is planted as a seed.

> **Leader's call-** Leadership begins to sprout.

> **Leader's preparation-** Leadership is tested as a plant.

> **Leader's position-** Leadership matures and bears fruit.

Paul gave this list for two reasons: first, to provide guidelines for churches to select leaders, second, to give church leaders a checkpoint for their own spiritual lives. Paul reminds us that if anyone aspires to be a leader, he aspires to a noble task. To have gifts and qualities and not take on leadership positions may be disobedience. The desire, however, must be accompanied by discipline.

The Qualities of a Spiritual Leader:

What sort of qualifications must church leaders possess? Paul lists the traits:

> *"Blameless…"* Am I quick to improve the areas that can damage my integrity?

> *"Husband of one wife…"* Am I loving my wife as Christ loved the church?

> *"Temperate, sober-minded, of good behavior…"*

Am I master of myself, that I may be a servant to many?

"Hospitable…" Do I exhibit a warm and welcoming spirit?

"Able to teach…" Do I consistently help others learn and become better disciples?

"Not given to wine…" Am I sober, watchful, and diligent so that I do not damage those who watch me?

"Not violent, not quarrelsome…" Do I have an approachable disposition that brings peace and healing?

"Not greedy, not covetous…" Am I allowing my leadership to be controlled by the rich?

"Rules his own house well…" Do I manage my own family before I try to manage the church?

"Not a novice…" Am I a seasoned, solid example for both insiders and outsiders?

RESPONSIBILITIES AND ROLES FOR SPIRITUAL LEADERS

Affirm the vision through prayer and discernment of God's voice.

Direct and affirm the values of The Gathering and the big picture of the ministry. What will the Church look like in five, ten, and fifteen years? What will The Gathering look like in five, ten, and fifteen years?

Determine the pace and values for the facility and finances.

Act as a discerning partner with the pastor. This includes theological, social, and community issues, as well as having a public position on key issues.

Ask productive questions and serve as a provider of solutions.

Bear the weight of decision-making responsibility for major business matters.

Serve as a prayer warrior for the general ministries of The Gathering.

Lead with a positive influence in the congregation.

Stay in close communication and offer wise counsel to the flock.

PROTECT YOUR PASTOR SO HE CAN PURSUE GOD'S VISION

One day you will stand before God, and one of the things He will ask you is:

> "Did you make it easier or harder for your pastor to fulfill the vision I gave him for The Gathering?" Find this thought very sobering and let it ground you in all your decision making as a leader!

So how do you protect your pastor?

> Help create an environment where he has enough room to work effectively.
>
> Make sure he has the resources he needs to pursue the vision. *(2 Corinthians 9:6)*
>
> Allow him to risk and occasionally fail for the sake of the Kingdom. *(Romans 15:1)*
>
> Provide for his family so that finances cannot become a distraction. *(Luke 10:7)*
>
> Give him sound counsel. *(Proverbs 15:22)*
>
> Gently push him back when he is wrong. *(Ephesians 4:15)*
>
> Defend him against careless accusations. *(1 Timothy 5:19)*
>
> Serve when asked and look for ways to improve The Gathering.

> Don't allow the people to tie his hands or chain his feet. *(2 Thessalonians 3:1-2)*

> Find the role where you add the most value. *(1 Corinthians 12)*

> Serve somewhere at The Gathering in addition to the eldership. *(Luke 25:24-26)*

> Lead and serve with eternity in mind.

As a spiritual leader it is your responsibility to maintain perspective, keeping in mind the bigger picture, not getting caught up in petty matters or territorial disputes. It is necessary to keep our hearts set on God, our eyes focused on the vision, and our minds engaged in thinking about what God wants us to be doing not only now, but ahead. It also means we need to be praying. One of the most important things you do as a spiritual leader is pray- for protection for the Gathering and its staff, for guidance from God, for confirmation of the vision that God has given to our leaders. We may not be that good at it, but we should constantly work at it.

Honestly, if you're not willing to really go after prayer for your church, then you probably don't belong in spiritual leadership.

Titus 1:5

Titus's job was to prepare leaders. Paul left Titus in Crete to do two things: organize the people and appoint leaders. **Strong leadership preserves what God does in His power.**

> <u>Choose</u> the men. How creative am I at finding new people to invest in?

Cultivate the models. How am I doing at turning my people into examples?

Create the ministries. How am I at creating ministry opportunities for new leaders?

Construct the management. How am I at monitoring them along the way?

Communicate the mindset. How am I at constantly keeping the vision alive?

Celebrate the mentoring. How do I encourage and celebrate growth?

LEADER DEVELOPMENT: FROM SHEPHERDING, TO DEVELOPING, TO EQUIPPING

Shepherding:	Development:	Equipping:
1. Care	1. Train for personal growth	1. Train for ministry
2. Immediate need focused	2. Person focused	2. Task focused
3. Need oriented	3. Character oriented	3. Skill oriented
4. Masses	4. Few	4. Many
5. Maintenance	5. Addition	5. Multiplication
6. Feel Better	6. Empowering	6. Unleashing
7. Immediate	7. Short-term	7. Long-term
8. Nurture	8. Mentoring	8. Teaching
9. What is the problem?	9. What do I need?	9. What do they need?
10. They begin to walk	10. Walk the first mile	10. Go the second mile

POSITION BASED UPON FUNCTION

Authority is not considered a position of privilege, as much as a responsibility to be used for service. Church government is intended to help us grow in our submission to the headship of Jesus Christ. In places where there is a good balance between liberty and controlled direction, very little government is needed.

When we leave our realm of authority, we depart from the grace that we have been given. This has occurred in our leadership team. When we become possessive, we will probably depart from our appointed realm of authority.

True unity is a unity of diversity, not conformity! Control demands conformity. This is Pharisaical religion!

The Holy Spirit, Who was given to each one of us, brought gifts and ministries to each of us so that every believer has a part in the overall ministry of The Gathering.

Those who are the most in touch with redemption and restoration are the most qualified to carry authority in The Gathering.

GOVERNING ELDERS

Read Numbers 11:16 and Acts 15 (Jerusalem Council)

Elders are to exercise governing authority in the Church. Governing elders are distinguished from those who are simply due respect for their age and faithfulness. Some have assumed that plurality implies that Elders are equal in authority, but in both Old and New Testament examples this is not the case. Before someone is appointed as a governing elder, we should be able to "see" the evidence of God's anointing on them. Should one who is appointed overseer of church finance have authority over children's ministry where he may have no experience or anointing? Elders may have wisdom for other ministries in the church, but one who is an overseer of the "gate" or ministry should not be able to dictate authority over someone else's sphere of authority. *(Acts 15)*

The inability to accept change is a characteristic of those who have become old wine skins. The Lord is seeking to prepare a wineskin that is perpetually flexible enough for the new wine He is bringing. God could have been more specific in making a clear outline for church government in the Scriptures. However, what He did give us makes and allows us to be dependent upon the Holy Spirit for many possible applications.

God does not anoint a position but a person! We can have all the positions covered, but if we don't have anointed people in them, we will be miserable failures at administrating The Gathering.

BUILDING A KINGDOM OF COMMUNITY

Read Matthew 16:18, 1 Corinthians 3:9-15, and Zechariah 6:11-15

1. The Church must build in harmony with God's eternal purpose. *Ephesians 3:10-11*

2. The Church must determine to choose the Word of God over tradition. *Psalm 138:2, Mark 7:13*

3. The Church must determine to be responsive to present truth. *2 Peter 1:12*

4. The Church must determine to build according to the divine pattern for the Church. *1 Corinthians 3:12-14*

5. The Church must determine to build to please God, not man.

6. The Church must place a high level of emphasis on the local church as the instrument that God uses to extend His Kingdom on the earth. *Ephesians 1:21-23*

7. The Church must determine to build up the saints on all levels. *1 Corinthians 14:4-12*

8. The Church must determine to strengthen all families of the Church. *1 Corinthians 16:15-18*

9. The Church must determine to develop and release the gifts and ministries of its membership. *1 Corinthians 12:14-25, Ephesians 4:16*

10. The Church must determine to structure itself with a biblical expression of team ministry. *1 Corinthians 12:28*

11. The Church must determine to exercise spiritual discipline relative to its membership. *Matthew 18:15-17*

12. The Church must determine to promote the biblical concepts of faith and sacrificial giving. *1 Chronicles 21:24, 2 Corinthians 9:7*

13. The Church must determine to focus on those things that promote the manifest presence of God in its gatherings.

14. The Church must develop house-to-house ministries. *Acts 20:20*

15. The Church must develop a strong corporate prayer life. *Acts 12:5*

16. The Church must determine to make unity a priority. *Psalm 133, John 17:11, 21*

17. The Church must understand the principle of servanthood and practice it inside and outside the church.

18. The Church must determine to take Christ's commissions seriously. *Matthew 28:18-20*

19. The Church must determine to maintain a first love experience among its membership.

20. The Church must determine to continue in an attitude of change and openness to further understanding and insight. **This is God-directed, biblically based change that is consistent with the nature and purposes of God.**

LEARNED LEADER OR NATURAL LEADER

Is all leadership innate and natural? Is all leadership limited to a spiritual gift? Is it possible that leadership can be learned? I am of the strong opinion that you can learn leadership! I have seen many, many people who don't fit the typical leadership image, emerge only to assume substantial responsibility, and carry it well. Not as a manager, but as a leader, someone who has true influence and utilizes it toward a clear and God-purposed future.

So, what about this person who emerges? Was there hidden ability and leadership capacity not yet utilized? Or were skills learned that enabled this person to function at a different level, a leadership level? Can someone actually begin to see life from a different perspective, the perspective of a leader? Or is this reserved for the few, the chosen, and the elite- those born with something special? Again, I believe you can learn leadership.

I do realize that different levels of God-given ability in things such as I.Q., discipline, charisma, drive, and personal energy play a major role. Some leaders are greater than others because of the task God has committed to them. This is clear. However, what we will look at here is whether you are a learned or natural leader, and how to make the most out of the purpose God has called you to.

The Learned Leader Characteristics:

Learned leaders have followers. This is the most basic characteristic that separates leaders from non-leaders. The requirement here is that people follow you because they want to, not because of your title. You may have a title, that is fine, but hopefully that's not why people follow you. The issue is not how many followers you have. It doesn't matter if you have five, fifty, or five hundred followers. The essential element is that people respond to your personal influence and follow your lead voluntarily. Non-leaders don't have followers. They may have helpers for a task, but that is not the same. Someone helping solely because of the task at hand, without engagement or response to you personally is not leadership. This is project-oriented management. Personal influence is essential.

Learned leaders must think leadership before doing leadership. Because leadership doesn't come instinctively for a learned leader, you must intentionally think leadership to remain engaged and effective as a leader. This is like the difference between a golfer with a natural swing and one who has to develop a consistent swing through lessons and concentrated effort to practice becoming proficient.

Learned leaders are not inwardly compelled to lead. This example will help you. If you are a learned leader and you walk into a room where there is a leader who is engaged, in charge, and things are working well, you will feel no real need or compulsion to take over. You will help if needed. You will most likely see how you can quickly be helpful, but you have no inner need or drive to take over. If, however, you walk into a room where there is no leadership- there may be a leader, but there is no leadership- and the environment is unproductive, unorganized, and the general spirit of the place is poor, you will rise up and do something about it.

Depending on your personality, skill level, and the occasion, you may do something yourself by taking over, or you may utilize your influence to get the right people doing the right things, but you will do something to get things headed in the right direction.

Learned leaders are industrious and take initiative. As learned leaders, you are likely to be highly productive and naturally migrate towards other highly productive people. You may sometimes be short on patience with those who appear to be flaky to you, you thrive on seeing things of value completed and are quick to take initiative to get things rolling. Seeing things stall out drives you crazy, your work ethic is strong, and you enjoy a full schedule.

Learned leaders seek results more than influence. This is subtle and can change over time as you gain more experience as a leader. In the beginning, you usually are more interested in getting it done rather than developing people around you. It is faster and easier and more direct. Natural leaders also want to get things done, in fact, they are driven by results, but they are more interested in increasing their influence with people than merely accomplishing the task at hand. It will be necessary for you to grow towards this model as well to be balanced.

Strengths:

Has passion and discipline. Learned leaders are driven, full of life, and purposeful. Personal discipline is often the strength that enables a learned leader to keep up with natural leaders and, on occasion surpass them.

Gets the job done. Learned leaders are generally fantastic at getting things done because of the balance between projects and measurable goals. As the learned leader continues to grow and their ability to work with people increases, their productivity becomes incredible.

Can mentor and teach leadership well. Learned leaders are great leader coaches for one simple reason. They had to learn leadership themselves, which enabled them to be good mentors and teachers of leadership.

Challenges:

Can lack confidence. In the beginning stages, leadership is not instinctive and confidence is often a struggle, sometimes causing you to second-guess your thoughts and decisions in general. With experience and time, confidence can build and will enable you to lead with great inner conviction and greater ability to inspire others as well.

May struggle to cast a compelling vision. This challenge is not about knowing and understanding the vision but communicating and selling the vision. Underdeveloped people skills and gaining leadership persona will need to be improved upon to get the people to follow your vision. It is completely possible. It does take time. Focus on your confidence first; win at leading yourself first before leading others. Know what you want and why you want it and at least partially how to get there, and then lead. You don't have to have all the details, but you must believe you can do it, and believe in what you are doing before others will follow.

Key Concept:

Stretching- Learned leaders always need to be digging, learning, and growing. It is absolutely essential to your success. Coasting is not an option. It is a good thing to feel as though you are in a little over your head. Humility and wisdom work together for the learned leader, as he stays focused and diligent as a student of leadership.

Psalm 78:72 "So [David] led them by the integrity of his heart and guided them by the skillfulness of his hands" (NKJV)

Application:

Consistent leadership exposure- you must have continual input of leadership development; serving in an environment that is proactive about leadership development will help ensure your success.

STAFF PERFORMANCE EVALUATION

Date _____

Name of staff member_____ Full time _____

Job title _____ Part-time _____

Evaluate staff member on the points below using the following criteria:

EXCELLENT – Well beyond expectations; extremely good
VERY GOOD – Perceptibly better than could be expected
GOOD – Adequately meets expectations
FAIR – Perceptibly poorer than could be expected
POOR – Unacceptable

Please rate each factor with a numerical value from 1-15 according to the following scale: (Put N/A if factor is "not applicable").

1 2 3	4 5 6	7 8 9	10 11 12	13 14 15
poor	fair	good	very good	excellent

Use numerical value:

   A. <u>Initiative</u>: Energy or aptitude displayed in initiation of action. _____

   B. <u>Punctuality</u>: Characterized by regular occurrence, being on time. _____

   C. <u>Attitude</u>: A mental position with regard to a fact or situation, a feeling or emotion toward a fact or situation. _____

   D. <u>Efficiency</u>: Effective operation as measured by a comparison of production with cost (energy, time, money). _____

E. <u>Effectiveness</u>: Producing or capable of producing a result. ____

F. <u>Ability</u>: Competence in doing, the quality or state of being able. ____

G. <u>Understanding</u>: The power of comprehending, that capacity to apprehend general relations of particulars (knowledge). ____

H. <u>Span of Attention</u>: Tenacity, perseverance, stick-to-it-iveness. ____

<u>Reliability</u>: Dependable, giving the same results on successive trials. (Dependability) ____

I. <u>Thoroughness</u>: Careful about detail, complete in all respects. ____

J. <u>Accuracy</u>: Correctness of work performed. ____

K. <u>Creativity</u>: Talent for having new ideas, for finding new and better ways of doing things, and for being imaginative. ____

L. <u>Personal Appearance</u>: The outward impression one makes on others. (Consider cleanliness, grooming, neatness, and the appropriateness of dress on the job). ____

M. <u>Drive</u>: The desire to set and attain goals, to achieve. ____

N. <u>Quality of Work</u>: Not only the amount, but what is actually accomplished. ____

O. <u>Stability</u>: Quality that enables one to withstand pressure and to remain calm in crisis situations. ____

P. <u>Judgment</u>: The ability to form an opinion, make an estimate or reach a conclusion when faced with a problem. _____

Q. <u>Flexibility</u>: The capacity to bend with change. _____

R. <u>Problem Solving</u>: Attitude to comprehend a situation and determine appropriate options for facilitation. _____

S. <u>Maturity and Growth</u>: Attitude and action taken toward personal and career improvement. _____

T. <u>Management</u>: Getting things done through other people.

_____

U. <u>Overall Performance</u>: The execution of an action, something continually being accomplished. _____

4. Please summarize how well the duties, responsibilities, tasks, goals, and objectives were completed. Indicate how much supervision was needed.

5. Major strong points:

6. Major weak points:

7. Were past goals accomplished? (Explain):

8. Goals to be accomplished:

9. Personal reply of employee:

_____   _____
Signature of Staff Member   Date

_____   _____
Signature of Evaluator(s)   Date

EXTRAORDINARY 21ST CENTURY LEADERS

What does it take to be extraordinary leaders in the 21st century? Leaders are always those who refuse to go with the status quo! Leaders are always those who realize that they are short on time and decide to seize the day!

Psalm 90:12 "So teach us to number our days, that we might gain a heart of wisdom." (NKJV)

Many young people fail to seize the day because they have been led to believe they have forever to make their impact. Satan is the great deceiver. Don't be fooled, if he can get us to become complacent or apathetic towards the things of God, he has won the battle. Each moment he can distract us is another life not being impacted with the power of the Holy Spirit. **We need to make our lives beautiful for God. We are the light of the world; through Christ Jesus, we are the world's only hope.**

Ephesians 2:10 "For we are God's handiwork, created in Christ Jesus to do good works, which God prepared in advance for us to do." (NIV)

Ephesians 2:10 "For we are God's masterpiece, He has created us anew in Christ Jesus, so that we can do the good things he planned for us long ago." (NLT)

We are to be excellent people, God invites us to walk in good works, awesome works!!!! Once you have had the opportunity to change a life through the power of the Holy Spirit, you will know in your heart that nothing else will satisfy, for this is truly the work the Father had in mind even before He created us.

There are four points I would like to discuss with you regarding leadership:

1. Be willing to raise the bar of excellence.

2. Be willing to learn quickly from setbacks.

3. Reignite your flame often.

4. Be intentional not evolutional in your endeavors.

Methods are many, principles are few; methods always change, principles never do.

*Psalm 78:70-72 He also chose David His servant and took him from the sheepfolds; from following the ewes that had young He brought him, to shepherd Jacob His people, and Israel His inheritance. **So he shepherded them according to the integrity of his heart and guided them by the skillfulness of his hands.** (NKJV)*

Notice when God called David, he was believed to be no older than 14 years old; Jeremiah, also called to a great work, was said to be 13 years old. You see, age really has no bearing on accomplishing great works for the Lord. The Lord said to Jeremiah "say not that you're but a youth!" *Jeremiah 1:5-10*

1. **Be willing to jump the status quo, be willing to raise the bar of excellence.**

   To become a great leader, you must do more than try; you must train.

   1 Corinthians 9:24 "Every competitor in athletic events goes into serious training. Athletes will take tremendous pains- for a fading crown of leaves. But our contest is for an eternal crown that will never fade!" (PHILLIPS)

   If you are going to be a leader you must train!

   To be a great leader, you must never stop learning; never stop growing. A great leader increases in knowledge and wisdom.

   Psalm 119:96-100 "Nothing is perfect except your words. Oh, how I love them. I think about them all day long. They make me wiser than my enemies because they are my constant guide. Yes, wiser than my teachers, for I am ever thinking of your rules. They make me even wiser than the aged." (TLB)

   To be a leader you must be a reader!!!!

   Proverbs 23:23 "Buy the truth, and do not sell it, also wisdom and instruction and understanding." (NKJV)

   Proverbs 10:14 "Wise people store up knowledge, but the mouth of the foolish is near destruction." (NKJV)

   Wisdom can be attained many ways; one way is

learning from our own experiences, which can be very costly at times. A second way is to learn from others' experiences; this is less costly and less time consuming. God gave us awesome learning experiences in biblical characters. He didn't show us every detail of their lives, just the experiences that would benefit us most- for about $50.00 (the cost of a Bible).

Where will we be in the 21ˢᵗ century if we stop learning now? Great thinkers say knowledge increases 20% every year. At this current rate, society reinvents itself every five years. If we don't keep learning, we will be obsolete in five years!! Don't be left in the wake of history, make history. *(Daniel 1:1- 2:49)* This is the main reason Christianity is not relevant to our modern society. We have failed to continue to grow at a rate comparative to the world. God does not want us behind. Daniel prophesied in the last days knowledge will increase. Believe it or not, he was speaking to God's people. You are the generation to make this change- GO FOR IT!

2. Be willing to learn quickly from setbacks.

We will all hit some speed bumps along the way, guaranteed! In Luke 17:1, Jesus Himself said it was impossible for offences not to come; we must realize someone is going to break our fine china. It is not a matter of if it happens, but how will we respond when it does happen? We have a choice to be bitter or better. If we trust that our lives are in the hands of the Lord, then we can rest assured that all things will work for our good. (Romans 8:28-29)

God's word tells us, *"For those God foreknew He also predestined to be conformed to the image of His Son, that he might be the firstborn among many brothers and sisters. And those he predestined, He also called; those He called, He also justified; those He justified, He also glorified." (Romans 8:29-30 NIV)*

How do we respond to setbacks? Do we realize we don't have time to become bitter or disillusioned?

Satan tries to assault God's character by lying to our minds. Has God really promised? Why isn't God taking care of you right now? If God loved you, He wouldn't have let this happen! **If Satan can cause us to stop and think on these lies, he slows down the process of God's work being accomplished!!**

A great leader has determined in his or her heart not to be hindered by disappointments, setbacks, or offences, knowing they have a limited amount of time to accomplish their vision. A great leader chooses to believe the best in every situation as 1 Corinthians 13:7 states *"love believes all things, bears all things, endures all things."* Decide right now, God is bigger than anything that may come your way!!

Psalm 37:23 "The steps of a good man are ordered by the Lord." (NKJV)

It is said that life is comprised of 10% of what happens to you and 90% of how we respond. What is your perspective? Perspective is based on and directed by your vision of the future.

Matthew 6:22-23 "The lamp of the body is the eye. If therefore your eye is good..." (NKJV)

How do we perceive the events of the life set before us? **Success? Opportunities? Or loss and negativity, leading to bitterness?** It is up to us.

Consider the tale of the two shoe salesmen:

> Once there were two shoe salesmen who sailed from America to Africa. When they arrived in the port of Africa, the first man got off the boat and saw that the natives in Africa did not wear any shoes. He immediately became discouraged and sent a telegraph back to America that read: "STOP the shipment of shoes, they don't wear shoes here." The second shoe salesman got off the boat, and when seeing that they weren't wearing any shoes, he immediately sent a telegraph to America saying: "DOUBLE the order of shoes, no one has shoes!"

We can look at our circumstances in a negative perspective, or a positive one, the choice is up to you! How do you look at your mistakes? You can't please God by playing it safe! **A righteous man doesn't give up, he gets up.** *(Proverbs 24:16)*

There are three kinds of people in God's kingdom: caretakers, undertakers, and risk takers. We must be willing to be risk takers to have our vision become reality! A righteous person always looks forward; our eyes are on the front side of our heads. *Philippians 3:12-16*

3. Reignite your flame often.

Revelation 2:1-5 "I know your works ... nevertheless, I have this against you ... "

Our love for Jesus is the most important aspect of our lives; nothing can substitute intimate relationship with Jesus. The two trees in the Garden of Eden represent works and life, religion and relationship. The enemy of our soul will continually see to it that we see in the same light that Adam and Eve did. We must not concern ourselves with works, but with pure relationship with God through worship and conversation. Our flame is reignited when we worship the Lord before His throne, true worship expressing love and thanks to God for all He has accomplished for us.

Worship and praise causes the Lord to manifest His presence. God dwells in the praises of His people. *(Psalm 22:3)* We must first love God and His people. *(Matthew 22:34-40)* Praise silences the enemy and stills the avenger. *(Psalm 8:2)*

When we praise God, we enter the highest form of humility, offering our lives to Him who deserves glory and honor. When we humble ourselves in worship to our Creator He exalts us to His place of residence, high above circumstance and issues of life that come to hinder our joy as His sons and daughters. Praise and worship create an atmosphere, a spiritual dwelling place for Holy Spirit to work and free us from the yokes of oppression. We are directed by scripture to put on the garments of praise instead of the spirit of heaviness.

Our flame, which truly does represent the life of God, can wane. Don't allow the enemy of your soul to condemn you; Jesus is the one who won't quench a smoldering wick. *(Isaiah 42:3)* A great leader is one who understands the primary call of God is simply to be with Him. Our heavenly Father truly does want our fellowship; He loves us and desires our friendship. He is so interested in our lives. What we consider minute and mundane He truly is interested in.

Never forget that good works stem from the life of God in us, they are results from the indwelling of Holy Spirit. A great leader is one who has come to fully realize that their flame is not truly theirs, but that which is dependent upon the infusion of the life of God. Those who burn out have forgotten this principle of reliance. A great leader is one who has learned to avoid the dry times, knowing they will eventually lead to a full-blown desert experience.

Flame igniters worship and praise. They fellowship with fellow saints and have a true love for the brethren. Flame igniters release forgiveness to others immediately. Giving our souls to the Lord on a daily basis keeps the flame of passion for Jesus ablaze!!

4. A great leader is one who is intentional, not evolutional in their endeavors.

Proverbs 29:18 "Where there is no vision, the people perish; but he that keepeth the law, happy is he." (KJV)

Vision simply defined is divine insight and guidance. Vision gives birth to hope, and hope does not disappoint because God has poured His love into our hearts by the Holy Spirit.

Most people die never having fulfilled their God-given purpose. I am convinced this happens because these same people never took the time or effort to get vision from God regarding their lives. This is so sad because it really is not too difficult to find the vision God has for us. I'm here to challenge you to be intentional. Don't be fearful!!!

Habakkuk 2:1-3 "I will stand my watch and set myself on the rampart and watch to see what He will say to me, and what I will answer when I am corrected. Then the Lord answered me and said; "Write the vision and make it plain on tablets, that he may run who reads it. For the vision is yet for an appointed time; But at the end it will speak, and it will not lie. Though it tarries, wait for it; because it will surely come, it will not tarry." (NKJV)

Make plain the vision God has given you, write it out, live it, breathe it, make it your all. Though it tarries, don't give up; it will come to pass!! Vision becomes our hope, our faith, our desire, and our reality. Vision is our gauge to determine progress (e.g., difficulties, success, and failure). Always cast vision, be a dreamer like Joseph who had big dreams.

A great leader is one who realizes not everyone thinks like him or her and refuses to allow the birds of the air to steal their God inspired dreams and visions. A great leader never quits pursuing God's plan for their life, knowing the relevance of their vision is God-inspired, God-sustained, and ultimately God-fulfilled. *(Ephesians 2:10)* A great leader refuses lengthy stays in the evolution and maintenance mode. They use the delays as times to seek the Lord for His counsel to improve, strategize, and tweak the vision, so that others may also run with the vision.

*Take time to meditate on the seven forces that flow from following God's plan:

1. **People with a sense of purpose find vision.** What goals and purposes do you see for your future, short and long term?

2. **People with a sense of purpose have discipline.** What bad habit or practice would you like to drop right now?

3. **People with a sense of purpose have God given esteem.** Find out what God has said about you.

4. **People with a sense of purpose have faith and courage.** What have you been afraid to pursue?

5. **People with a sense of purpose have resources.** Are you trusting God to meet your needs, spirit, soul, and body?

6. **People with a sense of purpose have drive and motivation.** Do you awake each morning with a desire to accomplish something?

7. **People with a sense of purpose have meaningful relationships.** Who in your life can you turn to for sound advice and counsel?

Stay on course and be intentional! Once we begin to see our vision, the next step is to stay on course with our vision. This takes moving with God, cooperating with His will, and being diligent to stay on track or run with the vision as Habakkuk declared. Remember the finish line is the goal. You may not have gotten a good start, you may be a slow starter such as myself, but our goal in the Christian life is to finish the course. *(2 Timothy 4:7)*

Here is some insight to the challenges you might encounter and how to help you stay on course and finish your divine purpose:

Satan - The greatest battles are fought in the mind: discouragement, fear, and confusion. What thoughts has the enemy placed in your mind that needs to be cast down?

Shortsightedness - Fulfillment of the vision does not come in a moment of time; sometimes it takes months, even years. Shortsightedness is like driving a car gazing only about 20 feet in front of you. It is impossible to get anywhere safely being shortsighted. Where do you need long-term vision?

Unhealthy or selfish desires - What are your desires? Are they God-given? Turn them over to the Lord, He will sanctify them for His use. *(Psalm 37:4)* Delight yourself in the Lord. Remember, desires can be fed and developed like our appetite, good or bad.

Love of money - What one area of your life could you sacrifice spending on yourself and give to God? Jesus and the apostle Paul warned us about how tricky money can be. We need money to do what God has called us to do. God wants us to have money and prosper, but He does not want money to have us. This is what caused the rich young ruler to lose his eternal purpose.

Ego and Pride - Pride goes before destruction and a haughty spirit before a fall. *(Proverbs 16:18)* Ego is a funny thing; it can make us think we are more than what we are or even less than who we are to be. Humble yourself to learn and grow and change. Truly then you will have expanded your horizons. In what areas is your ego a potential problem? Your looks? Your talents? Your intelligence? Give your ego or lack thereof to God and allow Him to use it to open new doors of growth.

Fear What are you afraid of? Change? Failure? Success? What fear is holding you back from God's best for your life? Keep your mind free from the fears and worries of everyday life! Input the Word of God! God has not given me a spirit of fear; but a sound mind, power, and love, that which prevails over all. We're to be anxious for nothing, because the Lord knows what we have need of even before we ask.

Proverbs 3:5-6 "Trust in the LORD with all your

heart, and lean not on your own understanding; in all your ways acknowledge Him, and He shall direct your paths." (NKJV)

Philippians 4:7 "and the peace of God, which surpasses all understanding, will guard your hearts and minds through Christ Jesus." (NKJV)

Isaiah 26:3 "You will keep him in perfect peace, whose mind is stayed on you, because he trusts in You." (NKJV)

God's plan for your life is tremendous, far beyond anything we could imagine. Yet it is His good pleasure to give us the Kingdom. Go for it! Give the Lord your very best and He will take care of the rest.

Editor's Note:

*Ken's original teaching on this subject was in regard to destiny. Later in life, he received revelation from God's Word that a believer should not rely on destiny or fate; rather, they are able to **know** the purposes of God for their life. Therefore, "the seven forces that flow from following God's plan" now reflect this revelation. For further study on this subject see Colossians 1:9-10 and Ephesians 1:17-18.*

RECEIVING THE SPIRIT OF THE FATHERS

Read Malachi 4:5-6.

We know this "Elijah" referenced here to be the prophetic move of God before the great and dreadful day of the Lord. Notice the turning, fathers to the children, and children to their fathers. Often, we hear of how the fathers must now turn to the children, but here we also find children turning to their fathers.

The fathers turning will cause revelation in the heart of the children and will bring the desire to be identified with their fathers. I see here a divine order. God, our Father, did not wait for us to turn to Him, but He first turned His heart to us.

1 John 4:19 "We love Him because He <u>first</u> loved us."

1 Corinthians 4:14-17 "I do not write these things to shame you, but as my beloved children I warn you. For though you might have ten thousand instructors in Christ, yet you do not have many fathers; for in Christ Jesus, I have begotten you through the gospel. Therefore, I urge you, imitate me. For this reason, I have sent Timothy to you, who is my beloved and faithful son in the Lord, who will remind you of my ways in Christ, as I teach everywhere in every church." (NKJV)

To receive the spirit of our fathers we must follow the faith of our fathers! To receive the spirit of our fathers we must be begotten of our fathers. Begotten means to allow fathering, to allow yourself to be brought to fullness and completion.

So many reading this may have the anticipation of receiving an impartation or some release of a mantle, to become better equipped, to increase their anointing...

This is all well and most likely good. Are we willing to follow the faith of our fathers? In no way do I advocate diminishing our uniqueness, nor do I desire to hinder the expression of the youth, or to restrict anyone's sense of purpose. I do want to remind us of the whole counsel of the Word of God. We are not only called to spread the good news, but we're also called to follow in the footsteps of the faithful. Listen to how Jude, the Lord's earthly brother, put it:

Jude 1:3 "Beloved, while I was very diligent to write to you concerning our common salvation, I found it necessary to write to you exhorting you to contend earnestly for the faith which was once for all delivered to the saints." (NKJV)

To accomplish God's purpose, we must first know God's plan. I see many today that are gifted, talented, intelligent, witty, and even great speakers! But the Kingdom of God is not demonstrated through any of those means. The Kingdom always has, and always will be demonstrated in power! However, please don't forget, it is not just the power to heal and do signs and wonders, but also the power to live by God's holy standards! **Presence, purity, and the power of God, in this order! Our fathers and mothers in the faith lived this way!**

This is what the Lord spoke to me, there have always been power workers. Pharaoh had them, Jannes and Jambres. Samaria had them, Simon the sorcerer. The reason Moses' serpent devoured the magicians' serpents was because Moses had left the holy mountain (where the bush was not consumed with fire) a different man, a consecrated man, a meek and humble man, a powerful man! The Lord said to me "Moses became who he was after the encounter with the Holy One of Israel."

Every place in Scripture, the words "Holy One of Israel" was uttered only by the prophets. The prophets were often referred to as father. A strong pursuit of God's holiness must define this move of God. Without holiness no one shall see the Lord. "Be ye holy for I am holy." *(1 Peter 1:16)* This means that the Lord put in place for us to achieve Christlikeness!

Fathers!! Jesus said to Phillip if you have seen Me, you have seen My Father. **We find this Christlikeness not only from Christ Himself, but from the fathers He places near us.** Fathers who emulate and emanate the Spirit of our Heavenly Father! **2 Corinthians 12:14-19** is a passage that opened my eyes and heart to identify true fathers in my life and how to connect to them!

Let's break this down, fathers:

Don't seek possessions, they seek people

Lay up for the next generation

Spend and are spent for others (Candle devours itself to give light to others)

Don't burden God's people

Don't take advantage of God's people; they utilize them instead of using them

Walk in the same spirit with you

Walk in the same steps with you

Don't make excuses

Do all things for the edification of others

To be begotten of our fathers we must:

Position our hearts to be like them. Imitate me just as I also imitate Christ. *(1Corinthians 11:1 NKJV)*

Live the spirit they lived. Paul labored and travailed until Christ was formed in the Galatians.

Give as they gave. *1 Thessalonians 2:8 "...Impart to you not only the gospel of God, but also our own lives..." (NKJV)*

Love as they loved. *John 3:16 "God so loved that He gave His only Son..." (NKJV)*

I'd like to close with an often-misquoted passage:

1 Thessalonians 5:12-13 "And we beseech you, brethren, to know them which labor among you, and are over you in the Lord, and admonish you; and to esteem them very highly in love for their work's sake. And be at peace among yourselves."

ABOUT THE AUTHOR

Ken Peters was the founding apostle over a network of churches that are called by the Lord to be part of a transformational movement to restore the New Testament model/pattern of the Church.

At an early age the Lord began to give Ken prophetic visions with tremendous clarity and accuracy. In 1982, Ken accepted the call of God, and began to move in the prophetic anointing. Ken served the Lord in ministry for over 35 years in various capacities, serving seven congregations. After many fruitful years in pastoral ministry, Ken and his wife, Tonja, began traveling full-time nationally and internationally as prophets, ministering the Word of the Lord to pastors, churches, and governmental leaders.

In 1999, Ken and Tonja founded Elijah/Prophetic Trumpet Ministries, an international ministry commissioned to build the Kingdom of God and bless churches abroad. In 2007, Ken and Tonja Peters founded and pastored The Gathering @ Corona, an Apostolic/Prophetic Reformation church. They assisted in planting and covering many Gathering churches throughout California and the United States and enjoyed leadership development, which eventually led to the establishing of The Gathering Network of Churches.

God placed a burning desire in Ken to see biblical apostolic/prophetic ministry restored and released throughout the entire body of Christ and to see apostolic government restored to the local church, the restoration of functioning five-fold ministers, training, equipping, and releasing the saints in their God given gifts to accomplish the work of ministry. Soon we will see the fullness of the body of Christ having freedom to cross-pollinate with the many streams of the manifestation of the Holy Spirit in the earth.

"The Power of the Sword Comes in Line with the Law of the Word" came from one of the first encounters that Ken had with the Angel of the Lord in 1984. While Ken was sleeping in a small, cold parsonage in East Bakersfield, California, a very bright light that filled the room with heat awakened him. As he woke up, he saw a magnificent Angel that began to talk with him and tell him many things. As he listened, Ken realized, "I better write these things down." He fumbled around and found a pen and scribbled out "The power of the sword comes in line with the Law of the Word," and went back to sleep. At the time, he didn't feel that he was able to capture what had been spoken to him, but when he woke up the next morning, he found it was handwritten precisely.

From that point on Ken became a studier of the Bible. The first time he read through the Bible completely was on a seven day fast. He locked himself in a hotel room with seven gallons of water, one for each day, and read it through in its entirety.

Ken's wife Tonja believes that first encounter with the Lord caused him to always be a studier of God's Holy Word, embrace the ministry of the Holy Spirit, and keep the balance of both.

Ken would never say he was a good leader; he would continually evaluate himself, especially when there were failures in our lives, children, friendships, or ministry fallouts. Tonja would watch him time and time again repent, humble himself, and press into the Father for needed transformation.

Ken and Tonja were married 34 years, and they were not perfect years, in fact they came with many trials in their marriage, family, and in ministry. The one thing that Tonja admired most about her husband in and through it all, he mirrored what Paul said, "...one thing I do, forgetting those things which are behind and reaching forward to those things which are ahead, I press toward the goal..." *(Philippians 3:13-14, NKJV)*